Ambassador Jolly Tanko Yusuf, C.O.N.

C.O.N. means Commander of the Niger.
It is a Nigerian National Honor, permanent, given to those who have served the nation especially well. Tanko received this honor for his service as Provincial Commissioner (Resident Minister) for bringing an end to the Tiv Riots in Benue State, during 1962–1965.

That We May Be One

The Autobiography of Nigerian Ambassador Jolly Tanko Yusuf

As told to
Lillian V. Grissen

Foreword by

His Royal Highness Mallam Gwamna Awa
Chief of Kagore, Nigeria

William B. Eerdmans Publishing Company
Grand Rapids, Michigan
Cambridge, England

Copyright © 1995

William B. Eerdmans Publishing Company
255 Jefferson Ave. SE   P.O. Box 163
Grand Rapids, MI 49503   Cambridge CB3 9PU U.K.

Library of Congress Cataloging-in-Publication Data

Yusuf, Jolly Tanko, 1923–
        That we may be one : the autobiography of Ambassador
Jolly Tanko Yusuf, C.O.N. / Jolly Tanko Yusuf : [as told to Lillian
V. Grissen].
        p.   cm.
        ISBN 0–8028–4139–2 (alk. paper)
        1. Yusuf, Jolly Tanko, 1923–. 2. Ambassadors — Nigeria —
Biography. 3. Nigeria — Politics and government — 1960–. 4.
Islam and politics — Nigeria. I. Grissen, Lillian V., 1922–. II.
Title.
DT515.83.Y87A3 1995   95–38879
327.669'0092—dc20   CIP
[B]

Table of Contents

Introduction

In this book, Jolly Tanko Yusuf, Nigeria's former ambassador to five countries in Europe, Asia, and Africa, shares his life, his vision, his passion.

Ambassador Yusuf's intimate involvement in Nigeria's political development since its independence from England makes him a person to whom we may well listen. He can be not only quiet and reflective but also bold and proactive. He is keenly aware of local and world-impacting events. Now a retired but very busy Christian citizen, he sees himself as a person whom God has chosen for a special purpose: to live and preach unity among Christians regardless of tribe or denomination. His accomplishments as both a visionary and a Christian leader reflect the bold approach he uses in solving political and people problems.

"I must speak. I must act. I have no choice. God had something in mind for me," he says. Christian elder statesman, politician, and diplomat, Ambassador Yusuf reveals a sharply single focus — devotion to his God.

The author, together with Lillian Grissen, speaks with a conviction born of experience and devotion to "his Jesus." Although he grew up in a strong, traditional Muslim family, he fought his father's demand that he attend an Islamic school. Beatings and chains could not keep the young lad from truancy and sneaky attendance at a local missionary school. When his mother could no longer stand her son's suffering, his father gave in.

As a 9- or 10-year-old, Ambassador Yusuf gave his life to Jesus Christ. He worked with leaders of the missionary community and with colonial administrators. When Nigeria became independent, his district elected him its first representative to Parliament. He rose to positions of national and international leadership, and sometimes served even during periods when the elected government was overthrown by the military.

Nigeria's political strife continues even today. Ongoing Muslim-Christian antagonism and conflict make his story relevant, even urgent. It reflects current conditions in Nigeria, which in turn typifies the chaos so rampant in many African countries muddling in the infancy of their independence from colonial powers and military dictators.

Ambassador Yusuf is a remarkable Christian. Lillian Grissen extracted from him — a very private person at times — many facets of his personality and character. She sees a quiet and reflective father and friend who demonstrates commitment laden with compassion. She portrays exciting facets of his life not known to many of his friends and the people he serves. She allows him to expound vigorously when occasion warrants it; he speaks out at both the injustice and discrimination so rampant today.

One truth — there must be unity in Jesus Christ — provides the compass for Tanko's Christian, tribal, and national aspirations. Unity is a mere word until the reader meets the person who has dedicated his life toward making that unity reality in Nigeria. Repeatedly in his exuberant quest he quotes Jesus Christ, "I pray ... that all of them may be one" (John 17:20).

He urges unity on three levels: in the Christian community itself, among Nigeria's more than 300 tribes, and throughout Nigeria's religious-political arena.

Ambassador Yusuf pleads, first of all, for peace and unity among his Christian brothers and sisters. Denominations, tradition, and tribal differences often hinder and hamper unity, he says. Christians are not organized politically, he laments. Denominations and sects do not trust one another. They are unable to agree on a candidate to represent them. Because Muslims know this, they bully Christians and get away with it.

Further, Ambassador Yusuf urges chiefs and leaders to settle inter-tribal conflicts peaceably. Having married outside of his father's tribe, he knows that differences in customs and traditions can be overcome. In the 1993 national election campaign, he travelled more than 65,000 miles in his personal automobile to visit villages, towns and churches and any place where groups would gather. He urges all Nigerian citizens, especially Christians but also Muslims and traditionalists, to foster unity among themselves and work together to develop a national structure in which all people can live with one another peaceably.

At a third level, he recognizes the threat of religious fanaticism and extremism. He pleads for better communication and understanding among politicians, elected officials, and government workers, both Muslims and Christians. He expresses outrage that the Muslim military have repeatedly interrupted the democratic process as Nigeria tries to return to civilian rule. He exposes the maneuvering and trickery of powerful fundamentalist Muslims who prevent the Christian community from participating in that process.

That's not all! Ambassador Yusuf also addresses a worldwide audience that has apparently not noted Islamic efforts to advance its beliefs and power globally. He fears the complacency of the western world. For example, he says, until the fall of the Berlin Wall the United States saw only Communism as its foe. But, he warns, the threat of Islam is far greater than that of Communism. The Soviet Union has changed; China and North Korea may some day change. But Islamic ideology will not! It cannot! It is bound by Koranic law and teaching, which are eternal. Islam's aspirations are worldwide and fanatic. It has an aggressive timetable for world domination.

Ambassador Yusuf has not allowed the Nigerian government to abdicate its responsibility to set up a governing system that allows both Muslims and Christians to live side by side, peaceably, and without discrimination. The battle, long and hard, continues, but so long as God gives Ambassador Yusuf strength, so long will he continue crusading for unity amid plurality. To him, a Muslim government ultimately dominating the Christian community is unthinkable. Both Christianity and Islam must be proportionately represented in a democratic government that must settle issues by practical and honest negotiation and compromise. Nigeria cannot stand if its government, through the machinations of fundamentalist Islam, is turned into a fascist, extremist, military dictatorship.

This story, easy to read and comprehend, can help Nigerian readers to enter the struggle and journey towards the Third Republic of Nigeria. It can help men and women of other countries to understand better the dynamics of Islam in Nigeria, in newly independent countries of Africa, and in the world. As an elderly father exhorts his dear children, so Ambassador Yusuf advises and encourages fellow Christians and countrymen and women. If Nigerians — Christians, Muslims, and traditionalists — can stop fighting among themselves and instead direct their energies toward promoting unity, they will have done their part to demonstrate that Nigeria can be an asset to earth's family of nations.

A Nigerian (TIV tribe) proverb, "U fegha, tso u due ken igbar," succinctly describes Ambassador Yusuf's philosophy. "If you keep struggling through the tall grass, you will suddenly come out into the open." If that opening does not come during Ambassador Yusuf's lifetime, it will ultimately come for him and all of us on that day when we will be with Jesus.

— **Dirk VanderSteen**
former Nigerian missionary
for the Christian Reformed
Church in North America

Foreword

Ambassador Jolly Tanko Yusuf is a forthright Christian, a politician, a diplomat and a courageous man of vision. I first met him in December 1956 when we both attended a joint session of the Northern Houses of Assembly and of Chiefs in the then-capital city, Kaduna. I discovered that the young Jolly — as he was popularly called — sensed then that something major and decisive was about to take place in Nigeria. The North and Nigeria as a whole were on the verge of slumping into a stupendous crisis. During this first joint session of the Northern Parliament (following the November election), Mallam† Yusuf (who later became Ambassador Yusuf to Germany, China, North Viet Nam, Korea, and Sierra Leone), I recall, then already exhibited his courage and foresight. Mallam Yusuf was an independent member from Wukari, and a Christian, in a Parliament comprised of predominantly Northern Peoples Congress (NPC) members. He noted early what has since always been the greatest threat to Christianity and the Nigerian constitution.

During the opening session, Mallam Yusuf challenged the decision of the Speaker of the Northern House of Assembly, Honorable Mr. C. R. Niven, to open the business session of the Assembly with an Islamic prayer. In so doing, the Honorable Mr. Niven was creating the incorrect impression that Islam was the one and only religious faith in the Northern part of Nigeria. Mallam Yusuf called the Speaker's attention to the fact that at least two or three religions were represented in the session. Would it not be only fair, asked Mallam Yusuf, that at least two different prayers — Muslim and Christian — be offered before the sessions began? The British-born Mr. Niven politely conceded. This event publicly marked the beginning of Mallam Yusuf's struggle against the championing of the supremacy of one religion over all others in Nigeria.

His vigorous, non-ending, and effective campaign against the Islamization of Nigeria eventually earned him two months solitary imprisonment in 1990 by Gen. Ibrahim Babangida, who was then Head of State. This

---

† "Mallam" is equivalent to the English "Mr." These words are used interchangeably throughout the book.

humiliation did not alter Ambassador Yusuf's convictions, as Gen. Babangida had hoped. No amount of adverse pressure or number of threats ever caused him to waver from his courageous convictions. During my long-time association with Ambassador Yusuf, I found him to be strong always, able to stand firmly by his beliefs.

At the request of many of his friends, he tells his story here for present and future generations of Nigerians and humankind. His book will hold you spellbound with vivid accounts of fascinating controversial issues and events that have produced the Nigeria of today. It may be one of the most important books about Nigeria you will ever read.

It will unravel the hitherto hidden person, Ambassador Jolly Tanko Yusuf.

— His Royal Highness Mallam Gwamna Awa
Chief of Kagore, Nigeria

His Royal Highness Mallam, Gwamna Awa, Chief of Kagore, Nigeria.

Acknowledgments

Few books are written without help. My story is no exception. Many friends have helped me.

My sister in the Lord, Lillian V. Grissen of Grand Rapids, Michigan, fashioned my original thoughts, made invaluable suggestions, and kept the purpose of the book in focus. My deeply loved friends, Lillian and her husband Ray, also provided a beautiful hideaway for me in their home, where she and I spent long uninterrupted hours discussing our different cultures, choosing words we hope will be meaningful not only to Nigerians but also to Americans and Europeans.

My trusted and loving family friends, Dirk and Jean Vander Steen of Hudsonville, Michigan, and Professor S.C. Ukoabi of Nigeria, read the draft and offered many valuable suggestions.

I cannot forget to acknowledge the youth groups and the various Christian leaders who urged that I should record my experience for the benefit of future generations and humanity before I go to my final rest.

I thank my dear wife, Comfort, not only for her patient reading of the original draft but also for her endurance, patience and encouragement during the many months I was involved in writing.

I also thank my mentors: Rev. Habila Aleyeindo; His Royal Highness Chief of Kagore, Mallam Gwamna Awa; Hon. Peter Achimugu; H.R.H. Malam Rwanikpan; Hon. E. B. Mamiso; and many others. Their support and encouragement brought about the formation of that very powerful organization, the Northern Christian Association (NCA) in 1964. They also moved me to think and concentrate on the problem of differences among Christian denominations and tribes. They inspired me to be mindful of unity in Jesus Christ, not only in teaching and encouraging Christians to rise above denominationalism and tribalism, but also in my conduct as a politician and diplomat.

— Ambassador Jolly Tanko Yusuf

Preface

I had not thought of writing a book that would criticize the corrupt leaders of the Nigerian government and the aspirations of fundamentalist Muslims to make Nigeria an Islamic country. But for some time now former colleagues, friends, and Christian leaders, including bishops and academics, have pressed me to tell the story of my life and the important events of my beloved Nigeria during my long career in public life.

Recently younger friends and associates have added their pressure on me to write not only about my life but also about the events that have been shaping our country since its independence in 1960. I am honored by these expectations, especially from today's young Christian adults. Not many Christian elders or retired statesmen and women have had the privilege I have had in serving Nigeria as both politician and diplomat.

In view of this, I will only throw some light on the development of my family as I know it and the role I played in our society, in particular, and in Nigeria, in general.

As an active participant in many of the events prior to and during Nigeria's independence, I am happy that I may contribute to the little knowledge that exists about this era of our history. If anything useful comes out of this bit of Nigerian history, credit must go to those who encouraged this exercise.

The facts of my public life can be found in a "Who's Who" reference book and in newspaper clippings beginning in 1957 when the name "Jolly Tanko Yusuf" was first heard beyond Mbarikam Mountain and across the River Benue. In addition, a little research in library files will provide details of the particular events in which I was involved.

It is not easy to write the biography of a man's life and public record while he is alive. It is even more difficult to relate one's autobiography. The main sources of my information are my diaries and notebooks, in which I have recorded events and my thoughts since 1942. Other sources include my late beloved mother, the late Pastor Istifanus Audu who was my uncle, Kawuy Magaji who died in 1982, and his sister NaHajara who is still alive. Hence there should not be too many mistakes. However, human nature being what it is, I cannot claim to be 100 percent accurate in reporting events, some of which occurred several years ago. Where mistakes exist, they are unintentional, and I hope the reader will forgive my human tendency to err.

I have watched my beloved country emerge from the throes of childbirth into infancy for more than three decades since its independence day. Just like a 2-year-old who tells his parents "No! No! No!" because he wants to be independent, so young Nigeria struggles. Although it no longer has to contend with imperial Great Britain, Nigeria now struggles against corrupt government and the determination of Nigeria's fundamentalist Muslims to make our country an Islamic state.

Nigerian citizens today want and need change. People want an honest, democratic government under which all citizens receive equal opportunity and treatment, irrespective of their faith and tribal origin.

Do Nigerians expect real change under the current circumstances? Many of us answer NO, but that doesn't have to be. I pray that my story will awaken Nigerians, especially Christians, to what is happening in Nigeria. Only then can we really pray for Nigeria. Of course, prayer alone is not enough. We must also act. A wise person once said, "We must pray as though everything is up to God, and we must work as though everything is up to us." Respect for one's fellow citizens rests in the knowledge that God created humankind in his own image. This belief increases our regard and concern for one another and one day will triumph over the madness that has overtaken our country.

In part my story is intended for my relatives and personal friends who are interested in the history of the Yusuf Ajiya Aluku family.

But, and this is more important, I pray that my story will speak to three groups: to Nigerian Christians who seek unity in Jesus Christ above tribalism and denominationalism; to all Nigerians who seek honest government, religious freedom, and equality for all; and to Christians in other countries that they may see that Islam's fundamentalist Muslims seek to control not only Nigeria but also the world.

Finally, I have written every page of this book with God in mind. If you are that individual to whom I have been calling for change, unity, and justice for all, I pray that God will change your thought and heart.

Islamic Threat — Nigeria and Abroad

Perhaps a nation should not be surprised at human suffering, neglect of youth, discrimination against freedom of religion, and a rotting government when an evil dictator supported by guns and tanks holds the reins of power.

For power is never satisfied; it grabs more and more.

And more.

Only the power of God is greater.

Nigeria is suffering. Intensely. Its gargantuan problem is corruption in government. It accentuates every problem in the land. Officials are more greedy for wealth than they are to serve the citizens. They use their offices and opportunities to multiply their comforts and increase their conveniences. Civil servants, many of whom use irritating red tape and unconscionable delays, enrich themselves with so-called "gratuities." Even military officers amass wealth at the expense of the common citizens. Without bribes, little is accomplished in Nigeria.

The greatest evil in oil-rich Nigeria is that millions suffer greatly. Thou-

Here, in Kaduna, Nigerians scrounge for scraps in rubbish heaps.

sands die of hunger each year. Until our government becomes humane and fair, Nigeria's situation can only become worse. Evil, shame-filled, is the government's glaring neglect of tomorrow's leaders, the Nigerian youth of today. Look at their faces! Graduates roam the streets for years and look for jobs. Why are they idle? Only partly because jobs are scarce, but mainly because Muslims have been handed the jobs that do exist.

Islam is using its dictatorial political power to bring Nigeria — every person and every institution — under the heel of Islam. Not only Nigeria, but also the world. Although Muslims today also are among the persecuted in some countries, e.g. Yugoslavia; to most people in America and Europe, Islamic worldwide goals seem far removed.

During one of my many visits to London, an Islamic scholar predicted to me — and vowed — that soon every third person in the world would be Muslim. He claimed there are already more than 850 million Muslims in the world. He said jokingly that almost half of this number lived in Nigeria, Niger, and other parts of Africa.

Western nations do not seem to notice that Islam is steadily advancing in their countries. Yes, multi-million dollar mosques are popping up here and there. No, this does not disturb the western world. Usually living among multi-ethnic populations with freedom of religion makes for a permissive attitude toward Islam. Indeed, one might generalize from the tragedy in Yugoslavia that Muslims worldwide are fighting for existence. Not so. One would think, though, that the awful persecution in Yugoslavia would make Muslims tolerant of all ethnic groups and religions. Not so. When they are in the seat of power, as they are in Nigeria, they become extremely exclusive. They believe Allah has called them to Jihad (holy warfare) against all unbelievers. The lull of complacency makes a fertile soil for subtle Jihad.

Any means — political power, military strength, oil and petro-dollars, vehicles, national aircraft and more — are being used to bring non-Islamic nations under Islamic influence and control. Currently, the Organization of the Islamic Conference (OIC) is using naira (the unit of value of Nigerian currency) and petro-dollars received from Nigerian oil and other resources to bring all Nigerians under Islam. Oil is its strongest weapon. The Islamic push for power throughout the world will not stop. Does not the Qu'ran (Koran) insist that all people must be converted to Islam?

The tentacles of Islam reach further today than at any point in history. Petro-dollars generate an unprecedented Islamic power not only in capitalist Europe but also in our beloved Nigeria. Corrupt leaders have so mismanaged our national resources they have yoked Nigeria as a member of the OIC, even though Nigeria is not an Islamic nation. Other leaders have even changed their faith in order to beggarly salvage their dwindling economy and retain political power.

Until the Berlin wall crashed in 1989, the western world, especially the United States, saw Communism as its arch foe. It fails to see that today Islam is the enemy. The western world should seriously resist any incursion of hard-line Islamic fundamentalism in their societies. The support that western powers gave to the Islamic world and the Afghan rebels on the grounds of chasing Communists out of Afghanistan surprised me greatly. Communism at least can be modified and changed, but Islam cannot. Witness the changes now occuring in the Russian states and even in China.

The western world fails to realize that Islam sees not only Christianity but also all western civilization as a threat. Sometimes I tremble when I ponder the complacency of the world's Christians regarding our common adversary.

Islam insists that no Muslim is answerable to a non-Muslim. Jihad remains a holy calling and appears in many forms in all spheres of life. Consider the world of business — unless a non-Muslim is converted he cannot be awarded any kind of contract. This holds true not only in Nigeria but also in many Islamic countries. Is it any wonder then that in Nigeria all positions of power, influence, and management are given to Muslims?

Many business people, including Christians in Nigeria and other parts of the world, in order to secure contracts in Nigeria, are caving in to Islam's demands. Islam is continually testing its strength worldwide.

In 1986 during one of my visits to Grand Rapids, Michigan, USA, I saw on television British and American converts speaking of their new Islamic faith. They intend, they said, to spread the gospel of "petro-dollar religion" in their own countries, the United States and Great Britain. Many Europeans, Americans and Nigerians who have secured employment in Saudi Arabia or other Middle East Arab countries have already been cajoled into becoming Muslims. Some become Muslims in order to retain their jobs; others who refused to be converted to Islam have lost their contracts.

Is the world aware of Islam's global growth? Its global ambition? Islam is no longer confined to the eastern hemisphere where capitalists can safely ignore it. All of western society is faced with the challenge of Islam; it is now on their doorsteps. Islam's objective, of course, is to bring the world under the umbrella of Islamic control.

The OIC is the Muslim common market through which Islam has tried to unite Islamic countries in the same way Europe is establishing the European Economic Community (EEC).

There is a difference, however. A big difference! Europe's common market was established for economic reasons. It is not a religious and political weapon to convert people to Christianity or to subjugate or eliminate those who do not accept that faith. Nor did European colonial powers use force to establish Christianity in their colonies. Muslim nations today, however, are uniting for the sake of the Ummah (the Islamic community). They use the vast international banking system that Arab and the Organization of Petroleum Exporting Countries (OPEC), including Nigeria, are building under the OIC umbrella.

President Anwar Sadat's trip to Jerusalem in 1979 and the negotiations that eventually broke the deadlock between Israel and the Arabs were regarded by Islamic fundamentalists as treason. Peace-loving people of all nationalities were stunned and grief-stricken when President Sadat was assassinated Oct. 6, 1981, by a band of Muslim fanatics hired by those who regarded the signed peace treaty his death-warrant.

Wake up, western world! To understand the OIC, one must understand the impact of petro-dollars on the world economy. International observers still remember the political and economic action taken by OPEC in the '70s — when Islam used OPEC in its attempt to force the civilized world to its knees. OPEC's attempt failed, but the western world's dependency upon Arab oil still exists. This gives Islam a potential hold over the western world's economic destiny. Arabs are gradually capturing control of the world's economic resources just as they took control of the world's energy in the '70s. Capturing the world, however, should not be by force, economic or otherwise.

Look around you! Besides mosques, Islamic centers are springing up everywhere in the western world. Travelers can see Islamic shopping centers in Central London, on Regent Street, Knightsbridge, and in other parts of Europe as well as in the United States of America.

Islam's illusion that it can conquer the whole world will likely end when desert oil dries up.

But desert oil will not run out soon.

Surely not in Nigeria's deserts. And it is here in Nigeria that God has placed me to do his work.

2

Looking Ahead ... and Back

Square One. That's where Nigeria is today as we near the end of 1995. Square One. Exactly where we were in 1966, when 6-year-old Nigeria had its first military coup. Square One.

Independent from England? Yes.

Independence from and for ourselves? No.

Nigeria's efforts toward stability have been sabotaged repeatedly since Oct. 1, 1960, Nigeria's birthday as an independent nation.

Why? How? People have not been allowed to practice and grow in independence and maturity because Nigeria's government, armed forces, and its powerful hard-line fundamentalist Muslim minority want absolute power only for themselves. Since 1960 no fewer than eight successful coups and counter-coups have made shambles of democratic, civilian government.

Since the early 19th century, Nigeria has been one of England's royal colonies, sending Nigeria's wealth to the mother country. It has ruled Nigeria with British governors and British militia. Using Nigerians primarily for labor and profit, it invested little effort in training Nigerians for positions of leadership and responsibility. Small wonder then that when England withdrew, Nigeria was not well-prepared to govern its more than 90 million people and the economy needed to support them.

The British left Nigeria immediately after granting it independence. Since the British left, the acquisition of personal power and wealth has been the chief occupation of Nigeria's rulers. Dishonesty and disorder have filled the vacuum.

In April 1993 excitement in Nigeria was running high. A cautious optimism, but nevertheless optimism, filled the air. Our country, after eight years of military rule under Gen. Ibrahim Babangida, was anticipating a nationwide election. Gen. Babangida assured the people that the June 12 election would be free and fair, and he would step aside. Citizens were excited — a real campaign to elect a national president was being waged in print, on the airwaves, in the cities, towns, and villages.

As the day drew near, some apprehension dented the optimism and uneasiness increased. Still, all the hoopla, campaign speeches, noise, and color of campaigning provided great excitement and anticipation. Observed even by other nations, the voter turn-out was heavy and glorious. Chief M. K. O. Abiola, a moderate Muslim from the Yoruban tribe, was elected. Such excitement.

But it was just a dream! A good dream with a horrible ending.

Gen. Babangida was stunned. His hand-picked candidate was defeated.

The next day, June 13, 1993, one day after the great election, Nigerians awoke to the usual warm equatorial sun. But our hearts turned cold quickly. Gen. Babangida, Nigeria's coup-commandeered president for the previous eight years, boldly announced on the radio that he had nullified the "corrupt election."

I was disgusted, but not too surprised. Angry, furious, and yes, shocked. What brazen audacity he had to, with a few words, wipe out the voice of Nigeria's millions. I had never truly believed he would relinquish his power. No longer controlled by a foreign country, we were now victimized by our own selfish and powerful leaders.

History is replete with accounts of political disorder arising from the manipulation of human gullibility by corrupt leaders. Nigeria, sadly, is no exception. Dictators cling to their power; they do not want to change for "the better." The beast in them makes them cannibals who delight in the mass suffering of the people they govern. Such monsters must be removed from office through organized mass action or by force if necessary.

Millions and millions of Nigerians who had voted in good faith shared my anger and dismay. They had looked forward to positive change in this first election since Gen. Babangida had seized the government eight years earlier.

Not every Nigerian shared our despair. It is an open secret that a powerful clique seeks to retain its grasp and grip forever, no matter the costs. A powerful group claimed Gen. Babangida's decision to be an "act of God." What profanity! Evil and injustice are the handwork of the devil. A cruel joke had again been played on Nigerians! Arrogant, corrupt and powerful leaders had made the people prey to their cunning.

What difference did it make to Gen. Babangida that President-elect Chief M. K. O. Abiola was from southern Nigeria, a "Yoruba man?" A great deal! Gen. Babangida and his corrupt cronies believe they must (and are the only ones who can) rule Nigeria. Only the few Fulani and the elite Hausa tribes, they say, have the talent, ability, and leadership qualities to rule Nigeria. It is their destiny! What arrogance! The truth is that their lust for power and wealth would be stymied if the honest election of a capable leader from the south, of the Yoruban tribe, of all things, were allowed to stand! Gen. Babangida's arbitrary, illegal nullification of the election proved my point.

Had he forgotten that south, north, west, and east are all part of Nigeria? Had he forgotten that some years earlier we had suffered a three-year civil war to keep Nigeria indivisible?

No, he remembered and was fearful. Gen. Babangida and his colleagues saw that the election threatened the current power structure and privileged position of the few, and he wanted none of it. He wanted no one from the South! No matter how capable, how honest, no one from the South would be allowed to jeopardize the power that lay tight in the hands of the military and its corrupt cronies.

It is an open secret that this powerful group of cronies will retain its grasp and grip forever at all costs, military or otherwise. And it will do so at the expense and to the distress of all Nigerians. This clique has a grand — and devilish — design! How long will it hold? Gen. Babangida's perfidy has seeded Nigerian hearts with rebellion, and what he has sown Nigeria will reap.

What will the harvest be?

Tragedy!

The harvest will be further disintegration of Nigeria, even chaos, unless Nigerian citizens, with Christian vision and leadership, unite and pool their effort and energy toward an honest government with equality for all citizens.

Gen. Babangida's hand-picked "interim president," Chief Ernest Shonekan, stumbled along until Nov. 17, 1993, when the "bloodless coup" of Gen. Sang Abacha dethroned him. Initially political observers and some supporters of Chief Abiola had hoped that the Kanori, Kano-born Gen. Abacha would sweep away the interim government, honor the June 12 election, and become the savior of Nigerian democracy.

It was not to be.

Hopes were dashed when Gen. Abacha, a cunning schemer, who had master-minded two military coups that brought to power Nigeria's seventh military ruler in 33 years, assumed power himself. Behind him was the support of zealous Muslims.

Gen. Abacha, however, has set up many Commissions of Inquiries into various governmental departments and agencies to recover some of the monies stolen by former government officials. We must continue to support his government as long as he continues to demonstrate this commitment to the well-being of Nigeria and his promise to hand over the office to a democratically elected president as soon as the wealth acquired illegally is recovered. If that could happen, the effort to return Nigeria to a path of viable democratic government and honesty will go a long way to instill discipline into the country's politics. Gen. Abacha should also shun sycophants and dubious, unintelligent elites who have been misadvising the governments of Nigeria.

Gen. Abacha, however, did not attain his position through a general election. We must not forget that the coup through which he obtained his office was nothing but a coverup to manufacture "reasons" to say civilians are not able to assume rule of Nigeria. That is why I am so disappointed. Abacha's "overthrow" of Ernest Shonekan (whom Gen. Babangida himself had appointed) was a bloodless coup to succeed him. Ultimately Gen. Babangida did not want to relinquish his power; he did not want to leave office. In his infamous "nullification speech" he said that he would "step aside." Clever, his word choice. "Step aside." Not "step down." This means that he can come back.

Yes, we are back to Square One — all the money for political reform (more than N200† million wasted!). Now we have not only the military regime, but also military governors in every state. That's exactly what we had in 1966. Yet this election fiasco may one day be a blessing — if we citizens wake up to what is happening, unite, and act!

It may surprise you that I — and many other Christians — had supported Chief Abiola, who himself is a Muslim. Because for three decades and more I have fought against tribal and religious politics and against an official or forced Islamization of Nigeria, I can understand that many people were amazed that I did support a Muslim.

History gives us many examples of formerly bitter enemies agreeing to not only forget the past but to work together. I think of the long and bitter animosity between Israel and Palestine, yet Prime Minister Yitshak Rabin of Israel and the Palestine Liberation Organization's (PLO) Chief Arafat have decided they must work together for the welfare of the people. It can be done, even though the path is rough and barrier-filled.

Surely, I reasoned, it would be better to support Chief Abiola rather than his opponent. If I had stayed home, refusing to vote at all, would that not really have been a vote for his opponent? Yes, Chief Abiola is a Muslim, but a moderate one. As a boy, he had attended a Christian school. He has taken studies in the Bible, so he knows what our Lord Jesus Christ teaches even though he himself may not subscribe to those teachings. During a meeting of Christian elders in Jos, he surprised us by leading us in the Lord's Prayer. He promised too to uphold the constitution of the Federal Republic of Nigeria, that Nigeria would not remain a member of the Organization of the Islamic Conference and that the law of our land would not be Sharia

---

† N=naira, the value of which fluctuates with the dollar)

(which is Islam's religious as well as civil law). He understands well that if the fundamentalist or fanatic form of Islam were enforced in Nigeria, moderate Muslims too would suffer. He realizes his own freedom would be jeopardized should fundamentalist Muslims gain absolute control.

With Chief Abiola, I reasoned, Nigeria would move forward toward freedom of religion. He would encourage Muslims, Christians and animists to live together peaceably. All Nigerians, even the animists, recognize a Supreme Ruler; we have that in common. For the Ibos, God is Chineke. For Jukun animists, God is Shido, And for the Tiv, God is Aondo. All Nigerians must be allowed to remain or become Christians, Muslims, or animists voluntarily — not by force or coercion, not by official decrees, nor by a political reward for accepting Islam.

Before we worry about our place in the world, however, we need to cleanse ourselves within. We will acquire respect only by what we are and how we behave and run our internal affairs. Unless we do, the outside world has reason to criticize us.

Christians and other Nigerians are deeply concerned about the country's momentum towards complete Islamization and the awful corruption in government whereby Nigeria is becoming a nation of poverty. We need to actively restrain the power that our rulers use so deviously. For one thing, unless we act, Muslims (even though they do not comprise a majority) will maneuver cooperatively to produce only Muslim presidential candidates, preferably zealous fundamentalists. Should that happen, our labors will have been in vain. Christianity and the telling of the Good News of Jesus Christ will suffer tremendously. Christians themselves will be humiliated and suffer great persecution and deprivation. We shall stand condemned before our Lord Jesus Christ and future generations if we do nothing.

What then shall we do?

We need to be united in Jesus Christ, but unifying Christians is not easy. Too easily do Christians pursue their own narrow interests, private or tribal. Too often they put individual or tribal goals above our communal mission to rectify the wrongs in our country. We Christians must work together and with others who seek honest government for all the people. Even moderate Muslims and other non-Christian groups realize that working with the Christian majority may be in the best interest of Nigeria.

For those reasons my continuous struggle for unity, first of all for Christians, unity that exceeds tribalism and denominationalism, will continue until my Jesus calls me home. My sadness about Nigeria is not unmixed with hope in God and trust in his control of all of life.

As I ponder what is happening in and to our country, I realize now more than ever that God has fashioned me, from my earliest childhood, to be an instrument of light and encouragement among Nigeria's Christians and among all who seek a unified and free Nigeria.

My pattern of behavior has developed from the time I became a Christian as a young child. Though Father and Grandfather were dedicated Muslims, they taught me many important values. I began to explore and experience the beauty, challenges, and demands of Jesus Christ when I became a Christian. The Lord said clearly to me that he wants me to imitate him. He has challenged me particularly to tell and promote that unity of which he spoke:

I have given them the glory that you gave me, that they may be one as we are one: I in them and you in me. May they be brought to complete unity to let the world know that you sent me and have loved them even as you have loved me. (John 17:22,23)

I believe this wholeheartedly. As he is one, we must be one. Always have the issues of equality and freedom of religion been part of me.

I have not changed.

As a Christian diplomat and government servant, and as a person who has been intimately involved in my country's politics since my youth, I see that God can and does use Christians to achieve his purposes.

I marvel at the path on which Jesus has led me since I was a young lad. He has directed my path since he became my Savior.

I look back. I see that long before I was born God had laid out his plan for me as I traveled this earth for him.

I cannot change.

Nor do I want to.

His hand has held mine tightly all my life. I see this so clearly, especially as I look back to my childhood, training, and opportunities to serve my country.

3

Firstborn Son

The birth of their first son on March 9, 1923, excited not only Father but especially Mother! I was that firstborn son.

Father's older brother, Mallam Mamman, already had two sons (Audu and Zakari) and a daughter (Mairemu). Up until my birth Father and Mother had three daughters (who one day probably would marry into other families). Now they had a son! An heir! Can you imagine the joy of my beloved parents? Parents saw children, especially males, as insurance for their old age. In addition, a son insured the continuity of the family name. Indeed, my parents were delighted with their infant son, the heir apparent! The naming ceremony, I am told, was a grand event. A great party. Many, many guests. Much good food: kunu (a light cereal), masa (a dish made of rice or maize), nakiya (wheat marinated in honey before cooking), fish and chicken, mangoes and plantains, and much more.

My parents named me Tanko, that is, "no son before me." When someone names you Tanko, it means that you are the first son born after daughters in a family and you have no brothers to help you defend the females in the family.

Jolly Tanko Yusuf's mother, Hauwa Yusuf, in this 1954 photo, denied herself much to provide for her children.

11

Mother was precious to me; memories of her are still vivid although she died more than two decades ago. Hauwa, my mother, was the daughter of Mallam Akedore and Madam Wati (Wakuru). They were members of an old, distinguished tribe, the Kpanzo, who were part of the Kwarrarafa tribe.

Mother's appearance reminded me a bit of a Fulani: light- colored skin and a pointed nose. She was lovely. I especially remember her laughter; it was generous and frequent.

Family is important to the Jukun and is not limited to father, mother, and children. One's love and obligation extend beyond the immediate family. Mother, for example, raised her younger sister, Na Hajara. Traditionally, the younger sisters — until they marry — help older sisters with the children so Na-Hajara played an important role in bringing up my sisters and me. No wonder concern for family comes naturally to me.

We children were close to each other in many ways. True, we did not have toys, parks, or children's playgrounds but we had the family compound. And, we did have story-time and story-tellers. After the evening meal, when the moon was shining brightly — on cool nights we had a fire — we gathered with our parents and brothers and sisters, and sometimes with uncles and aunts and cousins. As we talked together stories just happened — stories about our families and ancestors, stories learned from other families, stories of the great wind-devil, the wizards, and the animals. The children all listened, usually to their fathers. In the absence of Father or our uncles, Mother or an aunt would sometimes delight us with their stories of hows and whys. Parents used stories to teach their children. Stories also helped to make the family close and to keep them together. Mother loved her children and prayed to God regularly for them. She denied herself anything and everything and denied her husband and children nothing.

Sometimes, of course, a boy must be naughty, but most of the time I was obedient. Sometimes I offended Mother by not coming back home on time — I would be too busy playing to think of home. I remember Mother telling me (Father died when I was nine or ten years old, and family circumstances had changed drastically) that I should not bring friends home to eat so often because she didn't have enough for them and for me, and she worried because I was thin. I replied, "Then I won't eat." Then I would run away, but she would come after me.

As I grew a bit older and more serious, God showed me, "Look, you have no Father now, and look how your Mother suffers. There isn't much money. You must work hard to help her." And I did. Oh, I loved her very much and sometimes I teased her. Even when I became the Provincial Commissioner and occasionally returned home, I would first go to her and sit on her lap, and say, "How heavy am I now, Mother?"

One memory, however, still hurts me. I recall vividly her anxiety when my sister Anakyo and I were infected during an influenza epidemic in Takum. We were both critically ill. I could hear Mother praying loudly that God at least save her only son. Sick as I was, I remember squirming and feeling embarrassed, because I knew Anakyo could hear Mother too. Of course, Anakyo would feel that Mother loved me more than her. Both Anakyo and I recovered, much to the delight of Mother, who herself nearly died before us due to her anxiety.

Fatima, another one of my sisters, died quite suddenly when she was about six years old. Sometimes I wish she were still with me. We were close friends; I was attached to her and she to me, much more than any of my beloved sisters who have passed away since Fatima's death. I loved Fatima so much I have named one of my daughters after her.

It happened when Father, Mother, Fatima and I were returning home from Mkar where we had gone for Father's surgery (appendix) at the Mkar Christian Hospital (then operated by the Dutch Reformed Church of South Africa). We had just descended the mountain when Fatima became very ill. Mother was alarmed and very worried. We stopped near Yandev. That night Fatima died. Malaria, the killer that took the lives of millions of Africans before the introduction of quinine, took my beloved sister. We wept.

Many members of my extended family died from malaria, so I can never be friendly with a mosquito. It is a terrible thing, the mosquito; it is very powerful. That is why I take Daraprim (an anti-malarial drug) every Sunday.

Although Fatima died many, many years ago, she has never left my heart. I grieve still. I dream that one day, if God spares my life, I will ask the governor for permission to build a private school at Yandev in honor of Fatima.

Mother, who lived for others always, died at age 77 on June 2, 1971. I was serving then in Sierra Leone as the High Commissioner (Ambassador) of the Federal Republic of Nigeria. By the time Sierra Leone's Ministry of External Affairs got the news, the postal workers were on strike. Ten days passed before I received the news. When I arrived home Mother, of course, had already been buried. My heart was heavy; her death saddened me greatly. I missed her. I still do. Always her selflessness inspires me.

Sometimes I feel I could have done more for Mother. My sister Anakyo, who was very close to Mother, told me that as Mother lay dying, she kept asking, "Where is Tanko? Where is Tanko?" The thought still grieves me today. She would so much have liked to see me once more. Until she could no longer talk, she kept asking for her son Tanko. She slipped away quietly, as though she fell asleep. When my sister touched her, she was gone.

Later I moved her body to a place of honor in the front area of my family compound. On her tombstone, I inscribed:

With a great and affectionate memory of our
dearly beloved mother who peacefully departed
this life forever on July 2, 1971. This day
you quietly left us to sleep, leaving us to
mourn a dear, industrious, and illustrious
Mother. Though you are dead, your memory lingers
on forever, and your loving care and maternal
concern for us will be cherished forever,
and your exemplary work shall be continued in
peace and tranquility.

A Proud People

I wish I could have known him personally, my grandfather. I would have been so proud of him. I was about three years old when he died in 1929 (I think), but I can still remember him vaguely. He was big, tall and very black. Hair covered much of his body. I can remember touching his beard and his hair; both were black, curly, and spelled strength to my little boy's hands. Grandfather was Mallam Ajiya Aluku, Sarkin Noma (leader of farmers), an important member of the Jukun tribe.

Grandfather also had great spiritual strength. He was a Muslim. His faith in and devotion to Allah, so I am told, guided and determined his life. Although I have searched diligently, I have not discovered a single written document left by Grandfather. What I know about him I have learned from my father, a few of Grandfather's old friends, and from a few others who remembered him.

People could not talk about Mallam Ajiya Aluku without mentioning that the spread of Islam in our area was due to his devotion and faith. In 1885 Grandfather built the first mosque in his home town, Takum, a thriving agricultural town that lies near the border of the former northeastern Cameroons. This mosque called believers to prayers for more than 85 years. It was replaced — on the same site — in 1978.

Grandfather's social status and intellectual ability are no secret. Among the Jukun he was the religious leader of his generation, a great scholar and preacher. He sought and received permission from various village chiefs to spread the Islamic faith to the inhabitants. He trained many Islamic converts to become teachers and missionaries of the Islamic religion. To spread Islam, Shehu Dan Fodio (a powerful Fulani Muslim who claimed to be a direct descendant of the prophet Mohammed) often placed his brothers or relatives in charge of an area to maintain Islam and continue to convert more people. In the Takum area, however, because he had no near relative to whom he could assign the task, he asked Grandfather to accept the responsibility. He agreed and did his work very well. Because of Grandfather's outstanding contributions, Shehu Dan Fodio awarded him the coveted green and white Islamic flag. This was indeed an honor!

Grandfather had at least 25 children, I was told, most of whom died in infancy. My father was his eighth son. I do not know how many wives Grandfather had, but I do know he also had concubines. Nigerian laws regarding marriage accommodate the various religions that exist in Nigeria. While Christianity permits one wife only, Islamic religion permits up to four wives besides concubines without limit. Men found it to their advantage to have more than one wife. Wives contributed much to the farm work, the family, and the comfort of the home. A good farm and many children were good insurance, not only for men, but also for women in their old age. The government does not take care of its old people. Another reason given for the tradition of having more than one wife is that it kept females from roaming about and becoming prostitutes.

On the other hand, the management of polygamy can be as difficult for the husband as being one of many is for the wife. The husband has to judge his wives' quarrels among themselves, and often they are not easily settled. Often a wife might run away, and then the husband must go to her parents and beg them to talk to their reluctant daughter.

Grandfather, in addition to maintaining his household, combined his Islamic studies with farming and trading, which provided the wherewithal for his family. Wealth was measured by the size of one's farm, the size of one's store of greens and food, and the number of one's children and servants. From the records and from sentiments expressed by elderly people in Takum and environs, it is clear that the late Mallam Ajiya Aluku, Sarkin Noma, and his children were of good middle-class stock.

A Sarkin Noma is one who has a very large farm and has many people working for him. Grandfather was comfortably well-to-do, but he did not limit his concern to his family. He did not permit hunger in the Takum area. When mouths were nearly empty, he allowed people to gather produce directly from his farm. Of course, there were not so many people in Takum at that time. Although Grandfather contributed much to the improved well-being of humankind, many people have confirmed that Grandfather was more concerned with the people's spiritual health.

In spite of his deep concern for humankind, this highly respected Islamic preacher also traded in human beings. I have not been able to determine whether he actually sold men and women for personal profit or as part of carrying out his Islamic faith. For him, the sending of people to slave markets in Sokoto posed no problem because it was acceptable in the Islamic faith. I have learned that he may have sent as many as 300 slaves annually to Sokoto (which lies more than 1,000 kilometers northwest of Takum) and Rabah.

Later in my life (1961), I traveled with Premier Sir Ahmadu Bello, Sardauna (second in command to the Sultan) of Sokoto, to Rabah, which lies about 20 kilometers upstream of Sokoto, on the opposite side of the same river where the Sardauna himself was born. Here I — a descendant of a person involved in slave-trade — met a few folks of Jukun origin, descendants of the persons Grandfather had sent to Sokoto a long time earlier. I felt bad. Seeing these people saddened me. My heart was heavy. I understood with my mind that during Grandfather's time slavery was generally an accepted part of the human race; my heart could not understand. I realized too why and how some of my people had been slaves even in the United States and other countries, but my heart shuddered. If human beings would only see each other as equal in the eyes of our Creator, I thought, slavery could never have happened. I longed for all people to recognize each other as equal, as images of God, created by him.

I employed a few former slaves who were still living on the compounds of the old families that had owned them. They have all since died, but I still can identify some of their grandchildren and great grandchildren.

Today Jukun Christians (of whom I am one) are among the thousands of Christian Nigerians who are seeking to unite their country and to help it emerge from centuries of colonialism to its rightful place among the nations of the world. They are guided by our Lord Jesus Christ who, praying to his Father, said, "My prayer is not for them alone. I pray also for those who will believe in me through their message, that all of them may be one, Father, just as you are in me and I am in you." (John 17:20)

Perhaps a brief history will show the deep roots of my people. The Jukun tribe, although no longer at the zenith of its glory, remembers with pride such leaders as Grandfather. Jukun history, as far as it can be traced, bespeaks a strong, united mini-nation. Today, however, the unity that has historically produced harmony within tribes must now promote harmony among all the tribes that populate Nigeria.

The name Jukun is derived from Pa Jukun (human beings). These people were the Kwarrarafa people (or Apa as claimed by the Benue Idoma tribe). The ancient city of Wukari was founded by Aku Katapka, the ruler of the first dynasty. He was forced in 1660 to move Wukari, the capital, to its present site (about 12 kilometers west of its earlier location) because of threats from rulers of the Fulani tribe. Wukari today remains the focus of pride of the Kwarrarafa.

The once powerful Kwarrarafa empire was among those that flourished and collapsed in Nigeria between the 11th and 18th centuries. Even though modern Jukun people are today concentrated in Gongola and Benue States, with the seat of the Aku Uka (chief) in Wukari, a great number of Jukun can be found along the banks of the Rivers Benue and Niger, where fishing and farming are their main occupations.

There are also tribes of Jukun origin in Pindiga, Gombe (Bauchi State), Biu (Borno State) and Wase (Plateau State). In addition, there are many ethnic groups in Nigeria (Alago, Idoma, Agatu, Ankwe, Battas, Kakanda, Igbirra, Kunabe, Migilas, and Arochuku) whose ancestors were presumed Kwarrarafa (Jukun).

So, one cannot restrict the name Jukun to Wukari alone. Certain unpatriotic people of the current generation, however, want the world to believe that they only are the original Jukun. These people, most of whom dwell in Wukari, have tried by claiming superiority to push many Jukun-origin clans (Ichen, Tikari, Jidu Chamba, Kutep and smaller groups) out of their legitimate Kwarrarafa family. But I continue to challenge them. We are equal even though we bear different names. To regard one's self or clan or people as superior contradicts our equality in the eyes of our Creator. I believe this attitude of superiority, similar to some Americans' attitudes towards Native Americans or African-Americans, is wrong.

According to Kano and Borno chronicles and confirmed by oral tradition, especially those of Kanuri, the Kwarrarafa or Jukun are the descendants of the Wapa, who originally came from Yemenin, a place then part of the Arabic Peninsula. These people first settled and founded the town of Kukawa, which later became the capital of Kanem Bornu. The settlement lay just west of Lake Chad, which borders northeastern Nigeria.

The Kwarrarafa were great warriors who knew the power of cooperation and unity. By the 16th century the Kwarrarafa Kingdom was a sophisticated state which by the middle of that century had successfully attacked Kano (some 500 kilometers north) three times, destroying it completely in 1711. They also attacked Zaria, Katsina and Gombe.

Meanwhile, the Hausa and the Fulani tribal empires, which had been gaining strength, made the Kwarrarafa the object of their conquests. The Hausa and Fulani eventually drove the Kwarrarafa south to their present Benue Valley site and other parts of Nigeria. The unity that had made the Jukun powerful enough to face and conquer places hundreds of kilometers away came to an end, and they became a marginalized minority. Evidence of their former greatness in the North remains only in the names of a few Kano wards and citizens, such as Tanko Yakase.

It is regrettable that contemporary Nigerian historians, apparently due to political reasons, are presenting biased pictures of events that occurred and things that existed prior to British colonization of Nigeria. History reflects this bias of its authors and not historical fact as recorded by earlier historians, both British and Nigerian. We of the Jukun tribe must wake up before modern historians write off the tribe that gave birth to such leaders as Mallam Ajiya Aluku and His Highness Atoshi Agbumanu.

Although I detest any tribalism that prevents the progress of our young independent country, I believe the honoring of tradition provides the roots of the stabilization we need as well.

A Goodly Heritage

I wish I could speak just once more with Father. I had disappointed him, I know. That I, his firstborn son, refused to follow Grandfather's and his dedicated Islamic footsteps had pained him greatly. He did not know, he could not know, that God intended otherwise.

I loved Father dearly and respected him as much as I loved him. He was quiet, too quiet at times. Father reminded me of Grandfather. Both were committed Muslims; both cared deeply for their families; both were respected in Takum and surrounding areas.

Takum was a long-established center of activities. During World War I, its people helped the Germans who passed through on their way to the Cameroons. The name Takum itself means "shoot and sound" and originated with the sound of the cannons. The Germans trained Takum people to help them. Takum folks also supplied provisions. The town became a communication center for the area, including Wukari, Donga, Katsina Ala, and, because of its proximity, the eastern Cameroons.

Father, like his father before him, cared very much for fellow human beings. He behaved like his father. Whenever we were eating and anyone would walk up to our house, Father would insist that we all eat together. Whatever he could do to help anyone, he would do. Neither Father nor Grandfather realized how much they had fashioned my young mind.

Family was very important to Father. He loved his children, of course, but especially his brother Mallam Mamman. The two brothers ate their meals together, sometimes even waiting several hours for one another to be together. I remember this well because Mother made me wait for them, and I became impatient because I was hungry.

Father also loved his sister Madam Hauwa, who was married to a Hausa Muslim. Along with her own children, she raised some of the children of both Father and my uncle. A common Jukun custom at that time was that a brother or cousin (if you were in a position to do so) would raise another man's children, at least for a few years. We took these children into our own family. We believed that often an uncle could raise a child better than could the parent because he could discipline the child more consistently than could the parent. I don't remember just when, but perhaps I was five or six, Father sent me to one of Madam Hauwa's sons, where I remained for at least a couple of years. Because Madam Hauwa's husband was a Muslim, we children learned early and thoroughly the teachings of Islam which, of course, pleased Father.

Besides his farm, Father owned a bicycle and a sewing machine, both uncommon and both symbols of status. I was too young to ride Father's bicycle, but he used it regularly. Father was not a tailor; he was a businessman. His sewing machine was an investment. He hired men to make garments for him to sell. He was not, however, wealthy and when he died Mother worked hard to care for her children.

When by reaching over my head I could touch my right ear with my left hand and being independent enough to walk alone on the footpaths, I was old enough to go to school. I don't know just how old I was, maybe six or so, when Father sent me to the Koranic school in Takum.

I hated the Koranic school, but Father insisted. To be truthful, I wanted most to be with my friends who were going to the Mission School. But in a way, I suppose, I sensed then already that I preferred Karatun Boko (Western education).

My intense desire regarding even my earliest education caused a tremendous problem between Father and Mother and between Father and me. Although he was quiet, I knew I was displeasing him; yet I continued my behavior. I didn't understand Father then, but I do now. But what happened is done. And I cannot be unhappy about it, because through the Mission School and its teachers I began to know the Lord Jesus Christ.

The Koranic school usually met in the evening, although some sessions were held in the morning. Teachers were poorly paid, and evening school gave them the daytime to work on their farms. Our "school" was conducted outside Mallam Zakari's compound or under the tree in a field at the Unguwan Hausawa (Hausa Ward) in Takum. We were required to bring sticks for the fire; if we didn't we were punished. Sometimes we were forced also to fetch water and firewood from the bush for the teacher's family. We had to carry a pan into the town and beg for grain and food — we called it "alms" — to bring to school for the teachers, and if we didn't we were not cooperating and we deserved punishment. (I was spared this embarrassment, because my Mother, recognizing my "beggar's pan," saw to it that I had the necessary grain when it was my turn.) If we were tardy and our class had already started, we had to learn that promptness was an absolute. A whip was the teacher's weapon for punishment.

We students were divided into levels or standards. The teacher cracked his whip on us if we did not answer a question correctly or well. When he taught us words or ideas, we had to repeat them to him exactly. If we couldn't or didn't, we deserved punishment. One of my teachers, Mallam Jibrin, who knew I didn't want to be in his school, was especially strict and stern and exercised little mercy. He frightened me. He didn't like me; and I didn't like him. This didn't help my situation.

Still my beloved Father insisted on the Koranic school. He could not understand my motives, and he was very unhappy that I was not interested in the Islamic studies favored by the rest of his family. My great and beloved Mother understood my fierce desire for Karatun Boko. She seemed to sense that it was the way to success. Although she knew that final authority rested with Father, she kept on talking. Her idea was to allow me to go to the Mission School or "catechism school," as it was called, but at a time other than the Koranic School. She tried to convince Father but with no success. In the Islamic faith, the father holds the power and authority in the family, and Mother could do nothing. I was sent to board with the teacher.

After about two years I received Mother's approval to revolt against Father's decision. That decision nearly broke their happy marriage. I started to run away to the Mission School, which was operated by the Christian Reformed Church of North America, and which was just opposite our compound. In fact, it was in front of my uncle's home.

Father made sure that two older students, Zakari and Maishera, stood by our house daily, to accompany me to the Koranic School. But I ran away from school, again and again. I soon learned that Father had given the school authority to chase and find me and bring me back. Kasimu and Yahaya, another senior student, repeatedly searched for me and eventually always found me. Together they tied me down as I struggled. They chained my hands and legs. Both boys were brutal, but Yahaya, now Alhaji (an honorary title given to Muslims who have made the pilgrimage to Mecca), was the worst. Kasimu (also now Alhaji) seemed to be more sympathetic — sometimes.

One night, with both legs in chains that were cutting deeply into my legs, I escaped, hobbling and clanging into the bush. My legs were bleeding badly. But, I took two stones and for hours chipped away at the chains. I wondered if I would ever get through the metal. Finally the chain broke! Then I went home. My bloody legs and hands made Mother frantic. The scars of the tight chains and the beatings remain to this day, and I have shown them to Yahaya, who is now my close friend.

When I ran home I always went to Mother. She fed me, hid me, or sent me to Grandmother. But each time I would have to go back to school, where I would begin immediately to plan another escape. Sometimes I ran to the Mission School; they understood my awful predicament. One person, Mallam Joel Imiri Wamada, especially helped me. He would check to see if Yahaya and Kasimu were waiting for me outside. If they were, I snuck out of the window. Sometimes that worked.

Mother always wept when she saw my cuts and bruises. It became too much for her. It was just such an occasion that forced Mother to leave her matrimonial home to live with Grandmother across the road. Mother's courageous, daring sacrifice made Father realize that he might lose both his son — who on one occasion was almost bitten by a poisonous snake in the bush — and his wife. Reluctantly he changed his mind.

But he grieved as would any devoted Muslim who watches his beloved son leave the faith. I did sincerely offer my apology to him before he died. Still I thank God for giving me Christ as my Savior even though I offended my beloved Father whom I respected and adored.

One incident of our father-son closeness stands out in my memory. When I was about seven Father took me with him on a journey to Donga. Donga, about 45 kilometers from Takum, was a two-day trip on foot. Father wanted to congratulate Chief Mohammadu Sambo Garbosa, who had just been appointed Chief of Donga. (Chief Mohammadu Sambo Garbosa II ruled the Donga Chiefdom for more than 50 years.)

As a boy, I carried my father's leather bag containing his personal effects and his gifts. The gifts included woven gowns and a leopard's skin for the friend who had been elevated to the high office of chief. Even though Father had a bicycle, he could not ride it to Donga because the roads were so bad. Traditionally, one or more persons accompanied the traveler to look after his day-to-day needs and to carry his baggage. Usually a father wanted his son to serve in such a role. Or, possibly it could be a male servant. On the other hand, if there were no son, the father might choose a daughter, even though daughters usually served their mothers. I was very proud that Father chose me and not one of my sisters even though I was only seven years old. I felt very close to him.

I did not know then that would be the last year my beloved Father would live in this world. He died in November 1933, not too long after our memorable trip. Father's death left the responsibility of raising the children to Mother, and as the firstborn son I assumed the mandate of caring especially for her.

The Potter and the Clay

Once my parents had settled the contentious matter of my early education, I became a serious pupil in the Mission School. Before that time, however, there had been many interruptions as Yahaya and others from the Koranic school continued to hound me, often coming to the Mission School to find me. I hid in order to escape arrest. Other pupils, especially Joel Omiri, continued to help me.

As did my classmates, I took learning very seriously. It was so important that I gave every minute to it. Vaguely, but surely, I sensed my great God directing my life. I was a piece of clay, and the divine Potter was already gently molding me, helping me to see his love through the love of many around me.

The Mission School at Takum was small but excellent. My first teacher was Mallam Fillibus Ashu, a dedicated evangelist who had come from Wukari to teach at Takum. The main purpose of the Mission School was evangelism, and Mallam Ashu was a good teacher and a kind Christian. One of his sons, Ibrahim, was my close friend, so I spent as much time in their compound as he did in ours. Mallam Ashu encouraged me in my studies and in my life, as did his children. He was a vernacular teacher who devoted his life to God and humanity. He loved children. With open-mindedness and generous love he embraced all his students as his children, and he included me. I and many Christians as well owe him and Mallam Haruna Angyu, who succeeded him, a great deal. Not only did they give us a sound moral education but also they pointed us to Jesus Christ. We learned early that even young children had to reckon with God in their lives. Little did our teachers know how God would build on the foundations they had laid in our childhood.

He and my uncle, Pastor Istifanus Audu (Mother's brother), both encouraged me in the way of Christ. Mallam Ashu and Pastor Istifanus were very good friends. When Mallam Ashu searched for land in the Takum area for his family, Pastor Istifanus helped him. It was difficult at that time to obtain land in the Takum town, and Pastor Istifanus, who knew Father had influence in Takum, asked him for help. How ironic that

Father should be asked to help the man who was actively leading me from Father's Islamic faith to a foreign religion!

Love as expressed by Father, Pastor Istifanus, and Mallam Ashu in those days differed, I think, from the spirit I see about me today. At least then love was expressed more spontaneously and openly. It had both a physical and spiritual side; it cared not only for the souls of others but also for their stomachs. As pupils, we were encouraged to go to Christian homes because Christians received us with warm and generous hospitality. (Although the Jukun were naturally hospitable, Christianity intensified their kindliness.) Is it that way today? I do not think so.

After six or seven years of attending the Mission School, a few of us sensed that we had reached the outer limits of our teachers' academic expertise. Often when they gave us a problem in mathematics, oral or written, and would show us the answer, we checked our work with theirs. We saw that often their answer was wrong, and we argued with them. We argued respectfully and diplomatically, but we demonstrated that our answers were right.

So far our education had been in the Hausa language, the vernacular trade language used throughout Northern Nigeria. The school had no grades or levels. One day I discussed our education this far with one of my Takum friends, Garba Finiyo, son of the Chief of Bissaula. Garba was then attending the Takum Native Authority School, and his experiences were similar to mine. Like my teachers, his teachers could express themselves

Jolly Tanko Yusuf, second from left, gathers with relatives from left to right, including his brother Danladi Usuman Yusuf, his cousin Polycarp Haman Istifanus, Yakubu Magaji, Amadu Usuman, Ifremu Dauda Angyu, Ibrahim Jauro.

only in the Hausa language. They could not teach in English. We decided it was time for us to move on.

It would mean leaving Takum because our area had no secondary schools. The nearest school was Makurdi, which lay some 175 kilometers away and across the Katsina Ala River. I discussed the plan with Mother, who supported me, albeit reluctantly and with pain. This was not easy for her. Father, of course, had already died, and life was hard for her. However, with tears flowing, she consented. How well Mother understood her dear son! In keeping with Jukun tradition, Mother told me to obtain the permission of Grandmother Be (as she was called in Jukun), who as long as she lived was the mother in the family. She too was very fond of me. Mother briefed her before we met together.

I left the next morning. About 4:30 a.m. in Grandmother's sleeping quarters, she held both my hands and spat on my palms, and offered me the blessing of being sent out. She accompanied her blessing with prayer that Almighty God be with me at my next school and throughout all of my life, and that God grant all that I wished for myself. It was always me that Grandmother and Mother thought of. Mother cried. So did I. How could I part from Mother? She was my life.

I could not help weeping when I last saw her turn her back away from me. It was one of the saddest days of my life. I would not feel that sad again until many years later in 1968 when I had to leave my youngest daughter Rakiya for months in a tuberculosis hospital in Western Germany. It was then that I, as a parent myself, could fully appreciate Mother's emotional turmoil. I felt that same awful, lonely pain again on the day I learned Mother had died.

Mother pressed into my hands a small bag which held some food, some yams, and a small amount of meat and fish that she had fried dry. The food would not perish, and it was meant to last me for several days. She also enclosed a bit of money, a loin cloth, and a pillow. She herself had woven the cloth for the pillow and had filled it with cotton. It was precious to me. It was so much! For her to give me anything was a sacrifice. Although Father had cared for her amply during his lifetime, a widow in Nigeria has nothing when her husband dies. The farm workers left and, of course, I too was leaving. Any money she had, she herself had earned. Life was not easy for her. I knew this, and yet I felt compelled to leave her to continue my education. Education was necessary; I could see no other way. The little I had learned so far had given me visions of future possibilities for Nigeria and for its people, especially Christians. Mother had devoted all her life to us children after Father's death. Not only had she been a loving Mother but also she had unusual vision and foresight. I owed her so much. How much, I did not realize then.

Garba and I headed for Makurdi, which lay on the other side of the River Katsina Ala. The bridge was impassable. It was the rainy season and the river was flooded and very wide. Both of us were frightened because neither one could swim, and the river was infested with crocodiles. A man at the riverside agreed to take us across the river in his canoe, but he demanded all my money and more. It was either the cloth or the pillow Mother had made. What a choice. I had to keep the cloth, I felt, so I gave him my precious pillow. It hurt to give away a gift from my Mother, but I had no alternative. If I could find that pillow today, I would pay 10 times its actual value to retrieve it for its memories of Mother.

It took us six days to cover approximately 175 kilometers from Takum to Makurdi. We rested little, except at night. The path was dangerous. We heard the lions and leopards, in the distance and sometimes, it seemed, very close. We slept in the villages where we stopped. As in Old Testament times, the people welcomed strangers. Hotels and motels were unnecessary then — and unheard of. Huts were always available for travelers; people were kind and human life was highly valued. When we arrived at a compound willing to extend hospitality, we waited in the zaure, a round hut in which strangers wait for the host's welcome. We usually slept on the bare floor in the zaure.

Today Nigeria is different. I see people on the street who need food and a place to rest, but hospitality to strangers is seldom offered. Unfortunately. Nigeria has money; it has been blessed with lakes of oil. The wealth belongs to us — Nigeria. To us — the people. A country's wealth is not meant for the pockets of a few; a nation's wealth belongs to God, to be used for its people.

When we arrived in Makurdi, we went directly to my cousin Madam Ladi, who was married to "Mr. Sunday," as I knew him. He was a driver for the United Africa Company (U.A.C.).

The next day Garba, who was Catholic, registered in the local Catholic school. Being a Protestant, I was reluctant and hesitated. I went instead to the Christian Mission School (C.M.S), an Anglican school, where I was accepted with the help of Mr. Sunday.

Only a few students were from the Northern parts of Nigeria, so I was seen as an "alien." Gone were my romanticized ideas about further education. I found life difficult. No money. No friends. A foreign language. I started to learn English immediately.

But what was worse than any problem I had at school was my situation at my cousin's home. I soon learned Mr. Sunday did not want me there. Living there was unpleasant. He had two wives, one from his native area and Ladi, from my culture. In Mr. Sunday's culture, one might have a visitor for a day or two, but permanent guests had to contribute to the household. Even though I carefully obeyed all his instructions, washed the dishes, and did other domestic chores, such as washing the clothes and fetching water from the river, I found life at my cousin's house rough and rocky from the beginning. I was a liability to them because I could not pay for my keep.

Ladi, pushed by her husband, began to shout at me. If I had to stay late at school to finish or correct my written assignments, I knocked on the door when I returned. I just stood there. Several minutes would pass before anyone would answer. Usually it was Ladi, and she would shout, "Why are you so late? If you keep on being so late, you will have to leave!"

I got the message. In less than a year I left. I asked Ladi to please give me ten shillings for a train ticket to Jos, for no train traveled direct to Gindiri. Reluctantly, she went inside her bedroom and brought seven shillings. I thanked her and took my leave and boarded the next train to Jos, which was then the easiest route to Gindiri. From there I headed for the Teachers' Technical Training College at Gindiri.

Gindiri was a Christian college, one of the very best in Nigeria. Would the college accept me? Although I hadn't applied, I did not worry. Gindiri accepted people with very little education. Its standards were considerably lower than those of colleges in England where, through private studies I had already completed several courses, although I had not yet taken my final exams.

I spent the next several years (1942–1949) at Gindiri. Its imprint and impact for good were permanent.

Gindiri

I hadn't applied for admission at Gindiri because I hadn't planned to leave Makurdi so quickly. No one at Gindiri knew I was coming, so I was happy to find a few students from Takum, including my cousin, Mallam Ishaku Istifanus Audu.

At that time Gindiri was a many-faceted college designed to serve both young boys and adult males. Only a few women attended; usually married, they were the wives of adult students. The Sudan United Mission had established the college earlier to train evangelists. Teacher education and technical training were added later. The missionaries had designed the college primarily for people of Nigeria's Middle Belt area, where Christianity was becoming dominant.

Qualification for admission to Gindiri was a solid moral foundation rather than an adequate academic background. It sought boys who did not steal, smoke, drink, or stray after girls. No matter how brilliant you were, if your reputation for good behavior was not excellent, you would not be admitted. The emphasis in the education and training was on Christianity, morality and the dignity of labor rather than on knowledge and theory. Students were discouraged from rudeness, even to one another. Sharp retorts were considered unseemly, unlike today when cutting retorts and rudeness are the rule rather than the exception. The school, of course, rested on the foundation of the principles Jesus Christ taught in the New Testament.

With the help of influential people and my cousin Ishaku, who was learning carpentry, I was admitted to the department of building technology. This too, I realized later, was God's preparing me for tasks I had not dreamed of. In each step of my life, he led me.

At this time the impact of World War II was being felt globally, and Nigeria was not excluded. The war forced the British government to mobilize its colonies in order to fight Hitler's Germany. Although money for the operation at Gindiri did not come from the British government but rather from private missionary organizations, funds for the operation and maintenance of the school became scarce. Apprentices were being trained by

European missionary technical instructors. The students helped with the construction at Gindiri and with buildings in other towns, and thus gained the necessary experience.

In fact, in those days, the technical students and the pastors were more respected than the academic students. Technology apprentices were required to combine their practical training with theory and knowledge in order to broaden both their building skills and academic horizons. Apart from the subjects involved, no difference existed among clerical, teacher, pastoral and the technology students. All were equal and treated as equals. We were united in Jesus Christ. This, it seemed to me, was the way Jesus intended his people to live.

Our daily schedules were identical; only the subjects were different. At 6 a.m. we had prayer, after which we picked up our hoes and proceeded to the farms under an instructor's supervision. After 9 a.m. breakfast we went to class or work, depending on our field of learning. Studies lasted until 3 p.m., with a one-hour lunch break. For technology students, classroom studies began at 4 p.m., continuing until the day's written assignments were completed. Most of us usually had to return to the classroom after our evening meal in order to finish our assignments. Nighttime light came either from the moon or an ignited cotton wick steeped in an earthenware bowl filled with palm or groundnut oil. The smoky light was barely bright enough for reading.

Our learning was broad, and the value of the variety and extent of our experiences stayed with me throughout my life, regardless of how or where I lived with my family. Generally speaking, we students produced much of our food, and prior to concentrating on academics, built most of our shelters, sewed our uniforms, and made our desks, tables and chairs. We also helped with office work and typed our papers. We learned everything involved in daily living, including cooking, laundry, and more.

Still, we did have time to play. My favorite recreation was football, which we played almost every Saturday and on public holidays. Saturday was a special day for students; we were allowed to go to the market across the Gindiri River. Our principal, "Baba (father) Bristow," as we fondly called him, persuaded the townspeople to change market day from Sunday to Saturday for the convenience of the students. Using his personal funds, he himself constructed a Bailey Bridge (a rope-and-chain pedestrian bridge designed by Englishman Sir Donald Bailey) across the river. During the rainy season, the river was high and at times wild, and Baba Bristow was concerned not only for the safety of students and workers who went to the town for shopping but also for the general public.

Baba Bristow became the principal of Gindiri around the time of my admission. To me, he was Christianity in action. Here was this man from a far country (Scotland), different skin, different culture — who gave up everything in his life for us in Nigeria. I remember when he got married. We had thought he would never get married, but suddenly he did. We were so happy when he brought his bride to Gindiri. But she did not live long. She died after only nine months of marriage. We were numb with sadness.

Baba Bristow invested himself in us. He invested himself in me. He deserved the name Baba; he was father to all his students, both young and old. He demonstrated this to us so vividly at the time of his dear wife's death. Classes were dismissed and the school closed for a few days. Weeping with grief for him, we students greeted him at his home. Baba Bristow surprised us. He encouraged us instead of our encouraging him. He spoke to us more as a father than as a young man weeping over the death of his bride. He called our attention to the comfort God had provided him.

Baba Bristow decided not to remarry. He used all of his meager salary (about 25 pounds per month) to run the school when the world-at-war situation worsened. He lived Christ. I marveled at his spiritual strength. God used him greatly in my life.

It was this same man, Baba Bristow, who named me "Jolly." Before I was accepted as a regular student, I had been playing with the other boys as though I were one of them. Mr. Bristow regularly inspected the rooms where the students slept. Sometimes he would even come to the playing field to chase us to bed. Sometime the noise of singing and dancing reached his house after 10 p.m., which was the time for quietness. One evening he found me with the students, laughing and joking with them as though I were a resident. (I have always laughed a lot.)

He heard me and asked me, "Who are you? Why are you here?" I replied, "I am Tanko Yusuf. But I will leave, I will leave, but truthfully, I want to attend Gindiri, but I have not been admitted — yet."

In that friendly voice I learned to love, he said, "Well, jolly boy, I am the principal. Come see me."

I knew then I would be accepted. And with such a friendly naming ceremony, I could not but continue to be called "Jolly," and since then "Jolly" has been part of my legal name.

W.H. Grow, head of the technical department, paid me a few shillings a week to work in his garden during my spare time. I made time for this because the money helped me with my expenses and enabled me to send some to Mother now and then. He also trusted me with his bicycle at Christmas time so that I could visit my family in Takum. Christmas was a festive time. But it was much more — it was time for Takum boys to return home (not only from Gindiri, but from everywhere, if possible). It was time for the family to reunite, a time of excitement and joy. I would visit with Mother and my family.

I started out happily, even though Takum was 300 kilometers from Gindiri. I would not have to walk or pick up a ride on an old and dilapidated truck, overcrowded with men, women (some with babies on their back), and children, all standing, squeezed together with chickens, pans, food, and other possessions. On my good teacher's bicycle, I was on my way home — until I descended a hill that lies between the town of Pankshin and Kabril village, which is about 68 kilometers from Gindiri. There a pack of heavily laden donkeys moved so slowly ahead of me that I could not avoid them. The collision damaged the bicycle, which made me feel bad, but outside of a few bruises and cuts, I was not injured.

W.H. Grow, in this 1993 photo, was one of Jolly Tanko Yusuf's teachers in Gindiri. Grow served as head of the Building Technology Program.

I pulled my bicycle to Pankshin and repaired it as best I could. What to do? The next day I suddenly — and providentially, I know — met a young Yoruba fellow who was taking his brother's pick-up truck to Shandan, a town on my way. He kindly gave me and my bicycle a ride.

Almost immediately I noticed he was driving too fast. He had never even travelled this road before and now he was speeding. I warned him, but he did not heed my words. Suddenly he lost control and we landed in a ditch by the side of the road. I was badly hurt; my skull was bleeding profusely from a deep gash, and one leg and arm were bruised. I did not know whether any bones were broken.

I lost consciousness; I dreamed I was in Takum. I heard my helper screaming. When I awoke, I managed to find my Bible, my tie, and one of my old gowns. I clumsily wrapped the gown around my skull and secured it with my tie to prevent the breeze from entering my brain.

Painfully I crawled to the road where I met some itinerant Fulani cattle growers. I asked them to help us. They were frightened. They knew how often travelers were attacked as they traveled Nigeria's roads. But when I begged for help in the Hausa language, they listened. They agreed to get help for us and said it was the only help they could give. I wrote a note on a scrap of paper to the British District Officer at Pankshin explaining what had happened. After a couple of hours he arrived in his car, picked me up, and together we went to where my friend was lying. He took us both to the hospital in Pankshin. The young driver, not badly injured, I learned later, was soon on his way home.

For several days the doctor believed I would not survive; he gave up hope. I lay between life and death. Almighty God saved me. I sent a message to Baba Bristow, and within two weeks he came to Pankshin with his motorcycle, on which two could sit quite comfortably. Like a father he took care of me. Such love he had! I believe even today that he did exactly what Jesus told his friends to do, that is, "to let the world know that you sent me and have loved them even as you have loved me." (John 17:23)

It was unthinkable, of course, that a boy from Takum (which Christians regarded and called Jerusalem) would not return home for Christmas. Imagine Mother's disappointment and worry when her much-loved son did not arrive! I knew how worried she would be but there was no way for me to contact her. Communication, always very poor, on this occasion was non-existent. I am sure that Mother, had she known of my accident, would have trekked to Pankshin, even though it was some 200 kilometers from Takum. I wanted to go to Takum after being released by the hospital, but I could not. Gindiri had very strict attendance rules. Mother did not learn of the accident until about six months later when one of the students from Takum went home and told her about it, assuring her that I was indeed fully recovered and that I would soon be home soon to see her.

The Building Technology Program took six years, because the students had to be qualified in all the aspects of building. After seven years (1942–1948) at Gindiri, I had only one year to go. I still had to finish a little course work and take my final examination to qualify me as a builder and as an instructor in building technology.

But before long my schooling was to be interrupted.

Responsibility

Mother had long wanted me to "settle down." For some time she had been uncomfortable with my being single; after all, I was now an adult. She was unhappy because most other young men my age (21 years) and nearly all my friends had already married and, even more importantly, had already become fathers. How would Father's name be continued if her only son did not marry? Many years had passed since Father had died, and the family had gradually drifted apart and seemed to have lost some of its stability. This troubled Mother greatly. Although I understood her anxiety, I wasn't eager to assume marital responsibility.

I was Mother's only son, true. I lived on the family compound and willingly cared for her. Since 1942, while a student at Gindiri, I had been sending a few shillings to Mother now and then, as she was at that time the sole breadwinner in the family. I had not yet built a house for myself and my future family. I wanted to complete my training and take my final examination at Gindiri before I married. I also thought I should have a motorcycle and a reasonable amount of money on hand. In other words, I wanted to be somewhat established before I took the responsibility of a wife and children.

In the Jukun tribe in those days parents arranged the marriages of their children, and I accepted that. Sometimes, when a compound is ample, a man brings his wife to his family's compound. I intended to do that. Eventually I built a house on the family compound. It is still there, although it should be demolished and replaced.

I finally gave in to Mother's persistence. She spent much of her meager money searching for a suitable wife for her son. Her first and second attempts were unsuccessful. The fathers of the girls forced their daughters to marry men the fathers had chosen — much against their daughters' wishes. The parents, I believe, thought that my dowry was too small and I was too poor to marry their daughters.

In December 1947, Mother arranged for me to marry Matan Fara. I agreed. Only to please Mother. I could not do otherwise; Mother meant that much to me. I left Gindiri and went to Takum to take care of the pre-marriage details Mother had arranged. Then Matan Fara and I were married. Within 6 weeks I returned to Gindiri with my new wife.

When my first son, Joseph, was born Feb. 13, 1950, I was overjoyed and grateful to my wife and to Mother who, of course, was delighted! A grandson! Finally she was relieved of her anxiety of continuing the family name. Wonderful blessing. A grandson!

Looking back, that year was indeed joyous, a year of progress and prosperity. Not only did I become a father, but also I bought my first bicycle (Phillips Super-Deluxe) at a cost of £13.10.00 (13 pounds, 10 shillings, British money), a tremendous outlay of cash for me.

Dec. 7, 1952 brought me an added joy (and expense) when my daughter, Christiana, was born. I learned quickly to carefully and creatively budget my L.12.00.00 monthly salary. With the assistance of the student apprentices who helped on my family's fruit and crop farms, I survived. Over the next decade five more children were added to our family: Abigail, Ruth, Deborah, Fatima, Rakiya.

I hadn't forgotten, though, that I wanted to finish my work at Gindiri, so although not unmixed with the joy of fatherhood, I felt my responsibilities were heavy.

This motorcycle was Jolly Tanko Yusuf's main mode of transportation in 1955.

Jolly Tanko Yusuf's oldest son Joseph,
son David, standing, and Abram, with
pacifier.

I also repeatedly postponed my goal to pass my Senior Cambridge exams (post-high school and pre-university exams) that I had also been working on. Passing the exams was a prerequisite to acceptance in the University of Kent, South Devon, England. After I was elected in 1956 to the Northern House of Assembly, I was determined that I would complete my preparatory studies, and I did. I was accepted at the University of Kent. Later I would spend time in England, working days and nights on my thesis, fulfilling other requirements, and boning up for examinations. Not until 1961 did I receive my diploma in public and social administration.

Life for Mother, as a widow in Takum, had become intolerable. Her sisters and her mother had died. My older sister, Anakyo, had married. Another sister, Adiza, was under the care of Father's married sister Mala who lived far away. I, of course, could not remain at home. So Mother was left with no one except my younger sister, Maimuma.

Mother moved to Wukari to be near other dear relatives. Her family was related to one of the Jukun ruling houses†, known as Kuhwa in Takum. His Highness Atoshi Agbumanu IV, a great man and Minister of State in Northern Nigeria, was able to provide her with the care I could

† A "ruling house" is one from which a chief is selected. A tribe for several reasons might have more than one ruling house. For example, polygamy. A chief may have several sons with different mothers. Or, a chief may die and his brother appointed, and then there are two "ruling house" — still of the same family. A chief generally is appointed rather than elected. "Kingmakers," that is, a council of four, five, ten or even more respected elders in the community who work together with the chief, select a new chief. From among the princes from ruling houses the king-makers select that man who they think will best rule his people.

not. His concern for Mother matched his concern for me: often people thought I was his son because even physically we were similar — like me, he was tall, big, and laughed a lot. He and I were very close; he died in my arms in a hospital in Kaduna.

I had seen too that Maimuma needed a challenge. Growing up, she was often naughty. She didn't come home on time. She got into mischief. She would fight with her friends. She grieved Mother. Maimuma had too much idle time. She was a little old to begin school, but I realized she needed an education. I could see that she needed to be kept busy, and what better challenge could there be than education? It was difficult to persuade Mother to release her, to let her go anywhere by herself. I explained to Mother why I wanted to take her, what Maimuma's future would be without education. My dear Mother demonstrated once again her love and her unusual ability to understand what was best for her children; she allowed me to deprive her of Maimuma. Because I was one of the older Nigerians at the Mission station, I was able to get her into the Christian Reformed Church Mission School at Lupwe in 1950.

I felt deeply rewarded when Maimuma, my naughty little sister, worked hard in school. After a few years she became very interested in teaching. I

Ambassador Jolly Tanko Yusuf is surrounded by his extended family which includes Iframu Dauda Angu, Ibrahim Magaji, Daniel Ishaku, Ibrahim Jauro, Ake Burba, Mallam Bako Abwa, Joseph Tanko Yusuf, Yakubu Magaji, Mrs. Obadiah Maimolo and child, Obadiah Maimolo and Ruth Tanko Yusuf.

sent her then to the Sudan Interior Mission (SIM) Science School at Asaba and later to Gindiri Teachers Training College where she received her diplomas. Today she is the owner of a secondary, primary, and nursery school about 10 miles from Gindiri.

Nor, in keeping with Jukun tradition, could I ignore the children of certain relatives who looked to me for help and advice. Even though most of them were not too concerned about the education of their children, I was. I persuaded some of them to allow me to send their children to school. In 1952 I sent Lawi, the son of my cousin Mallam Danjuma (whom my Father had raised) to school. In 1953, at the request of Na-Hajara (mother's younger sister), I sent Na-Hajara's son Ahmadu Sule to school. Na-Hajara had taken care of my sisters and me when we were little children and I wanted to take care of her son now.

Even though I traveled much in my later work for the government, I accepted my responsibilities as parent to both my sisters, my half-brother Danladi (son of Mother's second marriage), and Lydia and Daniel (children of my cousin, Ishaku Istifanus, who was brother to me). Danladi was about six when I sent him to school at Lupwe. Later I sent him and Daniel to St. Paul's College in Wusasa for their secondary education.

Family has a narrower meaning in the Western world than in Nigeria; there the children are usually in a family of one father and one mother. In Africa the family extends far beyond that. We of the same blood are one family. Love, concern, and even parenting extend far beyond the immediate family of father, mother, and children. My mother and Mallam Ishaku Istifanus' father were sister and brother, born of the same mother and father. So Ishaku was my brother. I give to him; he gives to me; he is my brother.

Daniel and Lydia were special. When they were young they were very attached to me; they were like my own children. I could never forget that Pastor Istifanus (Ishaku's father) had helped me to accept Jesus Christ as my Savior and Lord.

Indeed, we were family — not merely by blood but more importantly family in Jesus Christ.

Lupwe

One more year and my training at Gindiri would be completed. I had married and my wife was now living with me. It was in 1948 that I received a message from the Christian Reformed Mission: "Please come to Lupwe as soon as possible. We need you to take charge of the Department of Works (the building department)." The senior Nigerian foreman who had been working for the Mission had been fired, and a replacement was needed immediately.

I was thrilled that I received this offer before I had even finished my training. Lupwe lies about five kilometers from my home town of Takum. I felt ambivalent, wanting to finish my work at Gindiri and being challenged to work at Lupwe. However, Rev. Edgar Smith, director of the Mission, had sent a letter to Mr. Grow urging that I be released.

Several questions entered my mind. How could I finish my training at Gindiri? Would I have another opportunity such as the one at Lupwe? Was it for this position that God had been preparing me? The work challenged me. After all, it was the work for which I had been preparing. This would

Jolly Tanko Yusuf, center, was in charge of the building department responsible or putting up the technical school at Lupwe where he also taught. The first class of students included, Idirisu Usman, Yakubi Ibi, Yusuf, Sabo Kuni and Gumbo Hassan.

be my first experience working in my chosen career. I reasoned too that
God directs every phase of his children's lives, and I had followed his leading this far.

I recalled fondly my earliest education at the Lupwe Mission School
where I had been led to know and love my Jesus. I wanted now to serve
him. I was young, 22 years old, and recently married. Inexperienced.
Would God be with me? Of course. Hadn't he led my life until now?

I accepted the challenge. I returned to Lupwe.

It didn't take long until I caught the vision of the missionaries. The need
for buildings was great. So far the missionaries had built a few houses for
themselves, but they sorely needed a chapel, school, dispensary, and other
buildings for their work.

Only one employee, my cousin Ishaku, who had finished Gindiri earlier, was a master carpenter. No others had even the minimum of construction skills. We even needed a driver. I soon realized that if the construction
were to be sound, solid, and safe we would need skilled carpenters,
masons, and plumbers. But very few men in the Takum-Lupwe area were
even acquainted with books. Very few were literate. Could they learn to
read plans and follow written instructions?

What we needed was a technical school, and we needed it pronto. The
staff agreed, and we began a school for apprentices. We taught the men to
read and write (in the Hausa language). How else would they learn elementary geometry, which they of course needed if they were to become
construction technicians? We introduced them to books and to building
plans. A gigantic challenge!

We realized that we had to recruit men who wanted to learn. It did not
take long at all to enroll our first four eager students. A small beginning. A
bit later a fifth student joined. We now had a solid core of apprentices.

Rev. Smith helped greatly, and God enabled the two of us to face the
days ahead together. Rev. Smith asked me to become Acting Manager of
Schools in his stead while he returned to the States for a six-month fur-
lough. This assignment included supervising the principals of the few elementary schools that already existed in the area. I felt like a jack-of-all-
trades, but certainly not a manager of schools. But, promised Rev. Smith,
an American teacher would be coming. Very soon, I prayed.

My workload was heavy. Each evening, in addition to planning lessons
and preparing a work schedule for the next day, I read handbooks on
school management. This was not the job for which I had prepared!

I was overjoyed a few months later when Mr. Gilbert Holkeboer, a white
teacher finally arrived from the United States. He became the Manager of

Schools. What a blessed relief! My responsibility as construction crew foreman and as teacher were enough for me. In addition, I had my family to
care for. But God again saw me through.

The dreams of buildings — churches, schools, dormitories — expanded as more American missionaries arrived. Rev. Smith himself was somewhat a jack-of-all-trades, and he contributed greatly to the development
of the Lupwe-Takum area. In April 1952, Mr. Ray Grissen and his family
arrived from the States. He became superintendent of all building construction and maintenance. I remained as foreman. He and I became very
close friends, brothers in Christ. Together we saw and helped the Christian

Reformed Mission expand to
and in many places, including
Baissa, Harga, Zaki Biam, Mkar,
and Wukari.

Relationships with some missionaries, however, were not
without difficulty. Sometimes
their behavior insulted my
workers and me. Their patronizing attitude reminded us keenly
of the haughty anti-black attitude that prevails among the
Boers in South Africa. We Nigerians did not like to think that
such an attitude also prevailed
in the United States. Any type of
racism, overt or subtle, is contrary to the basic principles that
the white missionaries themselves were teaching us.

It bothered us that some of
the missionaries taught us one
thing and practiced another.
God does not discriminate, they
said. The apostle Paul made this
clear when he said, "There is neither Jew nor Greek, slave nor free,
male nor female, for you are all
one in Christ Jesus" (Gal. 3:28).
Nor is there black or white, we
reasoned. How then could mis-

*Ray and Lillian Grissen with their chil-
dren, Kenneth, Donna and Susan, became
friends with Jolly Tanko Yusuf after Ray
Grissen arrived in 1952 to become superintendent of construction and maintenance at the schools in Lupwe.*

sionaries — who taught us about Jesus Christ as the Savior of humankind
— not regard us as their equals, regardless of our color — or theirs?

We longed for the "we" attitude of brotherhood — we Nigerians and
British and Americans — all Christians working together to spread the
Good News of our oneness, our unity in our Jesus. The maigida (boss) usually addressed us as "you," and seemed to limit his conversations with us
to work orders. Do not equals share love, hospitality, friendship, and com-
munion in Christ? Was it our color?

My American friends, Ray Grissen and later Mr. Ray Browneye, treated us
as equals. They believed and demonstrated that above all we are human
beings, all created in God's image. We worked closely together. We ate
together. We prayed together. Hunted together. Shared together. Fellow-
shipped. We became dear friends, lifelong friends. In fact, it was Ray Browneye who encouraged me to accept my first political appointment in 1957.

Are we Christians not one in our Jesus? Thoughts about unity in Christ
— or rather the lack of it — began to trouble me. My interest in unity
among and of Christians throughout all Nigeria was awakened while I was
serving in the Department of Works of the Christian Reformed mission at
Lupwe. My assignment had involved working with missionaries, church
leaders, and entire communities in Benue Province where the Sudan United Mission, Christian Reformed Church (SUM-CRC) had its stronghold.

I didn't realize at the time how great a part of my life would be spent trying to develop the idea of unity in Jesus among Christians in Nigeria —
regardless of denomination or tribe.

Jesus Christ himself had prayed for unity in his high-priestly prayer:

> I pray also for those who will believe in me through their message,
> that all of them may be one, Father, just as you are in me and I am in
> you. May they also be in us so that the world may believe that you have
> sent me. I have given them the glory that you gave me, that they may
> be one as we are one: I in them and you in me. May they be brought to
> complete unity to let the world know that you sent me and have loved
> them even as you have loved me.
>
> — John 17: 20-23

Christ's words became my passionate desire, the driving force in political life. I yearned that we Christians be one in Christ.

Gradually I was becoming more aware that if such unity were to
become ours, something had to be done about the denominational differences that white missionaries had brought with them from their home
churches. The damage being done by the white man's emphasis on

denominational doctrines, styles, and practices deterred the progress of evangelization in the northern part of Nigeria.

As Christians, we needed no encouragement in that. Unless we moved beyond our differences, the rapidly growing churches, Christian schools, health and educational facilities that the missionaries were establishing would not serve our Lord, Christian communities, and Nigeria. And, when Nigeria would be independent — as I believed it would, one day — we Christians would need to be strong and united. Tribalism would be a strong factor to overcome, and denominationalism would make unity in Christ even more difficult.

I realize too well that differences among churches and people do exist, and one cannot subscribe to all the beliefs of all denominations. People and churches do interpret the same Bible differently. God created us in his image, but with different gifts and interests. Some folks are academic, professional, higher educated, wealthier — I could name many more differences — but these are not differences of color, which to us seemed to be the main difference between us and white missionaries.

For example, I recall a particularly unpleasant encounter with the maigida. It happened at a time my crew was building the a clinic. The maigida had instructed the craftsmen, including older men like Mallam Yamusa, to carry very heavy equipment to the site, a distance of about four kilometers from Lupwe. To me, this seemed harsh and unfair. As it was at that time, my crew rose at 6 a.m. daily for prayers. They then had to go to the home of the maigida and his wife to do gaisuwan maigida (prostrating one's self while greeting a superior person, as was the custom). After all this the men would finally set off for the construction site and a day of hard work, carrying very heavy construction equipment. It was too much. It was very humiliating to me.

On that particular day, it happened that I, on my bicycle, came up behind Mallam Yamusa and Mallam Garba who were struggling to transport a heavy, primitive block-making machine to Gidan Tamiya. I became very angry. I raced ahead and found several young, strong laborers whom I sent back to help the men carry the machine to the site.

The following day after gaisuwan maigida and morning prayers, the maigida requested me to see him in his office. During the encounter I told him pointedly that he was wrong to force older skilled craftsmen to do the job of much younger, unskilled laborers. My impertinence infuriated him.

He shouted, "I've seen you reading those Communist newspapers. That's where you get those strange ideas. Now you want to spoil my people, who have been working for me for years without complaint."

I waited for him to calm down. Meanwhile, my crew, waiting outside, was terrified. They could hear the angry shouting inside. Some of them were shivering; they were afraid we would all be fired. How dared a very young black man (me) argue with a white man, a missionary, a maigida, no less. They didn't know then that I was defending them. I didn't want my men to go on strike, but I was determined that if the situation were not rectified, I at least would refuse to work.

Yes, I was young to be talking like that to an older person, but I knew that the maigida knew that if I left the job at that time, no one else was qualified to do it. I walked out, and the men went to Gidan Tamiya. Later that day I went there to see the men. They had done did very little work that day, however, because none of them knew how to survey. Only the maigida and I could do that. At the end of the workday, they reported to the maigida that I had not been at the site so they had been unable to perform their work.

The whole day was wasted.

But was it?

The next morning the maigida told me to come to his office after morning prayers. I went, but I did not observe the usual gaisuwan maigida. I entered his office, removed my hat, and said, "Good morning, sir." He ignored me and kept looking out the window.

Ten minutes passed before the maigida revolved his chair toward me. "Why didn't you work yesterday?" he asked.

In 1950, Jolly Tanko Yusuf was allocated this hut in Lupwe by the Rev. E.H. Smith.

"I would rather be sacked than continue under the prevailing conditions, where my staff is not respected, their welfare not protected, and my senior men are not treated humanely," I replied.

Again he threatened me. Again, and yet again. I did not budge. I stood there. Firm. Silent. Finally he agreed with me. Yes, the skilled workers and the laborers are human beings and they should be treated with respect and dignity.

I said, "Thank you, sir," and left.

I went to my crew; they were very surprised that the maigida had not fired me. I spoke to them about their dignity and worth. "We must be obedient," I told them, "but we must not give up our rights as human beings; we should not be treated as goats. To speak our minds is not sin; it is not against Christianity." We discussed some of the maigida's patronizing behavior toward us and agreed we should speak to him about it when necessary, but we must speak politely.

It was a major step forward for me and my workers. Many disagreements followed, of course. But from then on the maigida listened sympathetically to my suggestions or advice. Sometimes he acted on them. He made many concessions to the workers, including a review (and increase) of their salaries.

This concern for my people was not new in my heart. For some time already I had sensed the implications of equality (or lack of it) for my people when the day of our independence and freedom from British imperial domination would come. And it would come — very soon. For so long had Nigerians been the objects of colonialism, their self-concepts were very low. I encouraged my workers to think of their own worth in God's sight; had God himself not sent his only Son to die for each one of us? Every human being, including each one of us, has been created in the image of God.

Although my mind was filled with thoughts of Nigeria's future, the political implications of equality both among blacks and with white men and women had not yet inspired the minds of many Nigerian Christian leaders. They were too busy criticizing one another. African priests and the few Nigerians working under British, Irish, and American missionaries quarreled continually among themselves. Had they not read Jesus' teaching about unity in him?

Meanwhile, Islamic influence in Nigeria was growing. Very, very few people concerned themselves with this phenomenon. Many people, including educated elites from Nigeria's south, believed there were no Christian communities of any size outside the Middle Belt areas (Plateau, Benue, Gongola, Niger, Kwara, and some parts of Bauchi, Borno, and Kaduna). Even Christians in positions or professions of importance — pastors, doctors, lawyers, government workers, university graduates — were ignorant of the strength of Christianity in the Northern part of their country.

In a way I could understand their complacence, but I realized too they had to be awakened to political reality. For several years already, as a young man living in town, I had listened to all speakers whenever they spent time in Takum. I observed how they had accepted the idea that the Muslims were in authority. The British too, I observed, having believed Muslim propagandists for several decades, proclaimed the Northern states as Muslim states. They encouraged all of Nigeria to believe it.

I observed too that Christians were not being placed in any positions of authority or power. Many citizens were unaware that a majority of Nigeria's civil servants and its military forces were (and still are) Christians. Once people accepted the false claims of the Muslims as fact, it wasn't easy to change their minds.

I did not know then how extensively this condescending and prejudicial attitude and behavior of the British would permeate the Muslims, tribal units, and people in power in Nigeria after it gained its independence.

Where would my deep passion for respect for one another and equality among black and white, men and women, Christians and Muslims lead me? I wondered how it would affect my life.

Seedtime

The Good News of Jesus Christ spread widely throughout Northern Nigeria during the first half of the 20th century. The Christian Reformed Mission of the United States officially entered Nigeria in 1940. It began its work in the Lupwe-Takum area of the Benue area among the Jukun and other tribes. It began as and is still a branch of the much larger Sudan United Mission, which had been founded in 1918 by an Englishman, Dr. Karl Kumm.

All of this was happening while Nigeria was still part of the vast British empire. The English government, with its capitol in London, used British and Irish people to help them rule its global colonies and protectorates. For this reason, white men and their wives, both missionaries and government workers, often enjoyed extraordinary authority in British colonies, much more than did Nigeria's indigenous people. I suppose this is natural — the government and the missionaries shared the same color, culture, and language. Nevertheless, these white-only privileges contributed to the insidious paternal and patronizing racism of many foreigners living in Nigeria. Missionaries were not immune.

Most of the British missionaries, in Nigeria at least, were appointed to various government statutory boards. Divisional Officers (D.O.) and Residents got most of their information — and advice — not from the Nigerians themselves but from the missionaries (who often had preceded the district officers into Nigeria by years, even decades, and who to some extent had learned the culture and traditions of the people). Rev. Smith, who married an American lady, Nell Breen, and who eventually became a naturalized American, served on several committees and even on the government's Education Board. By virtue of these positions, he served as advisor to the government and kept it informed as to the goings-on among the people.

Many missionaries also adopted the government's haughty ways. Not consciously, perhaps, considering their cultural affinity. During the early '40s, for example, when some missionaries "trekked" to small outlying villages, they were carried on litters by laborers. To us it seemed like that mode of travel would have been more appropriate for British royalty. The carriers were not paid; rather, missionaries tipped them with a pence or two, a piece of soap, or perhaps a piece of candy. Nor were the villagers paid, even though they provided most of missionaries' food — chicken, fruit, vegetables, and eggs. They too were tipped.

It became clear to us that the missionaries' personal cooks and stewards were as important (to them) as were governmental secretaries or senior civil servants! So important to the maigida and his wife were the servants that they were given food even before the nurses. At that time we had professional, hospital-trained male nurses but white missionaries did not realize how important they were to us — much more than they themselves or their personal servants. And last, after everyone else had been fed, we builders were given food. We were humiliated.

Do not misunderstand! It was not that the missionaries did not care about our people. They cared very much — or they would not have come to Nigeria to tell and demonstrate the love of Jesus Christ as Savior and Lord. But, it seemed to us, they did not practice what they taught — that through the blood of Jesus Christ we have unity, oneness. Their patronizing and niggardliness bothered me. Somehow they regarded us as different. They did not understand us. Of course, there were tremendous cultural differences between us, but more than that they seemed to see us as less than themselves. That is how we saw it.

My people were very, very poor.

And in our eyes missionaries were very rich.

They imported most of their food from the United States or England; what food we had we grew ourselves. They had too much; we had too little. Yet, certain missionaries, when they knew that supplies would soon be coming for them, either burned or destroyed their extra food rather than sharing it with the poor. The reason, they said, was that "Blacks should not have that kind of food." Why not? I do not know; I cannot imagine. They did the same with extra clothes they had brought. We had very little clothes; could we not have used these clothes?

I witnessed much of this myself while I helped my cousin, Mallam Danjuma Musa, steward of Miss Bertha Zagers, one of the early missionaries. As a young boy, my friends and I would wash the pots and pans in return for "crumbs" and empty tin cans and bottles. We sold them to the people in town, mimicking the missionaries who did the same. One missionary nurse, Miss Anita Vissia, was a pleasant exception, and she at times was unpopular with the maigida. She never sold anything, and often gave of her food and other necessities to my people.

During the 1950s as Nigeria began to move slowly towards independence, missionary lifestyles began to change. Some of the wives themselves began to cook for their families, and the missionaries ate more African foods. Many missionaries began to treat us as equals.

But it was a very early missionary who saw us as "black diamonds." No statement of Christian Reformed involvement in Nigeria can be made without mentioning Miss Johanna Veenstra, an S.U.M. pioneer missionary in Benue Valley. She was a member of the Christian Reformed Church in North America but not sponsored by it. Wakwaki Veenstra or "big woman" — as she was lovingly called — was her popular name. She was a big person, not only physically, but also spiritually. She was big in kindness and love for the people. She lived Christ.

Though the work of Wakwaki Veenstra was terminated by her early death in 1933, her challenge to the people of the Benue Valley has been passed on unforgettably through her writings and stories. At the time of her death more than 100 people were attending worship services every Sunday in the Lupwe area alone. To me, this said unmistakably that God's purpose was to establish his church in our area, Islamic mosque and Grandfather's ministry nothwithstanding.

It was Miss Veenstra who persuaded Dr. Karl Kumm, a pioneer missionary of the Sudan United Mission, to plead with the Christian Reformed Church in North America to consider the Africa that lay south of the Sahara as a possible area in which to halt the spread of Islam into Africa's heartland. Would Nigeria have such a Christian stronghold had Miss Veenstra been less vocal? I wonder. Through her efforts and those of a few other Christian Reformed missionaries, the possibilities of evangelism in Nigeria were explored. Rev. Lee Huizenga and Dr. J. C. DeKorne, two veteran missionaries who had served in other countries, came to Nigeria as representatives of the Christian Reformed Church. They surveyed the opportunities, found them exciting, and urged the CRC to adopt Northern Nigeria as one of its mission fields. In 1940 the Christian Reformed Synod formally, through its existing mission in Benue Valley, became a member of the Sudan United Mission.

Until then the Sudan United Mission had operated around Ibi, Wukari, Wase, and other northern areas. The number of Christians to whom the missionaries ministered then was not large — only 49 in all, the fruit of more than two decades of planting. That foundation was solid, however, and remained; it encouraged Christians to become involved in political activity in later years.

During the late '40s Nigeria's longing for independence slowly became more vocal, and between 1949 and 1960 this voice expressed the confused political consciousness and aspirations of the people. Christians, firmly grounded in God's Word, joined the dialogue.

The ground was fertile, the seed rich, and the planting continued, and the harvest continues to be plentiful. Miss Veenstra's work did not die; God had already taken care of that. Miss Nell Breen, who had been Miss Veenstra's colleague, continued the work. It was about this same time that the young English missionary, Edgar Smith, who worked for the S.U.M. in the Ibi area, wooed and won young Nell. Two other missionaries, Miss Jennie Stielstra and Miss Bertha Zagers, completed the group that carried on during the 1940s. In 1945 the first Christian congregation was organized in Takum, and by 1947 ten new outstations had been opened.

Among the first Africans in the area who accepted Jesus Christ were Baba Habu and Mallam Fillibus Ashu. Both became evangelists. Mallam Ashu had come to Takum from Wukari. If I had a godfather, and if I would have had a choice, I would surely have chosen Mallam Ashu. Through his exciting story-telling and eloquent evangelism he introduced me to Jesus Christ. Mallam Ashu was a father not only to his own children but also to all the children around his compound, especially me. He and my uncle Rev. Istifanus Audu (one of the longest serving pastors in our area) taught me to know Christ. Through them I came to accept salvation through my Savior Jesus Christ and to give him my life. All in all, I praise God and thank him for the work not only of the Christian Reformed missionaries themselves but also of the many Nigerian evangelists they trained. Our country has been and today continues to be blessed through the many churches and schools they established.

We who attended the Mission School were taught that as disciples of Jesus Christ we are his witnesses always. The missionaries taught us how to preach the Gospel. We were given the opportunity to practice preaching in nearby villages.

Although I worked full time with Ray Grissen in the construction department of the Mission, the idea of helping the Kunabe people continued to pop up in my mind. So many children and no school! People without basic services — water, roads, dispensary. Sometimes it moved me to tears. I wanted to make their lives a bit more comfortable. Kunabe was a very backward area.

In December 1951, I went to Kunabe with one of my closest friends, Mallam Enoch Audu Ibrahim. Together we laid the foundation of both a church and a school. Today they are the hub of the many thriving churches, elementary schools, and even a secondary school in the Kunabe area.

One time Ray Grissen and I went to the nearby Lissam worship service; Pastor Daniel had invited me to preach. After the service we went to Kunabe. There Mallam Adamu Kunabe† welcomed us. The Chief of Kunabe also received us warmly and granted our request to preach in his village. Within just a few minutes 16 persons appeared from the mountain side. The Chief instructed them to listen to the sermon, which I spoke in Jukun. The Kunabe people listened carefully. However, they found it hard to lay aside the idols that they worshiped and received the Gospel with little enthusiasm. Mallam Enoch Audu Ibrahim persisted with the work in Kunabe and in time many came to know Jesus Christ as their Savior.

As the children and adults in our area began to learn how to read, the lack of books bothered me. I determined to at least make some Christian books available to them so that they might learn about my Jesus. I built a bookshop (which included a postal agency) in Takum. In 1954 I sent Mallam Bako Abuwa to the Sudan Interior Mission (SIM) bookshop in Maiduguri, Borno province, for training. Many people enjoyed the bookshop while it was open. However, mismanagement caused the bookshop to falter; after about three years I had to close it, and the government took over the post office. I was sorry to see this ministry fold.

A great event for the local Christians during the '50s was the transfer of the mission of the Dutch Christian Reformed Church of South Africa to the Christian Reformed Church. The Dutch had established a strong church among the Tiv. The political climate in Nigeria was changing rather rapidly during the '50s. I believe too that the South African missionaries sensed that our pending independence from Great Britain would change their status greatly in Nigeria. The South Africans were simply not as acceptable to Nigerians as were Americans.

Although the DRCM missionaries behaved reasonably well, they were still South Africans, and we Nigerians deplored the attitude of white South Africans towards black South Africans. That same attitude appeared often in their relationship with Nigerians. South Africa's system of government at that time contrasted sharply with the democratic government we anticipated for the coming independent Nigeria. Not only the Muslims and many people in our then-British government but also we Christians believed these people should not be in Nigeria. Concerned Nigerian Christian leaders approached the DRCM and unofficially suggested they either give their work to the Christian Reformed Church or possibly be asked to leave Nigeria.

To avoid the awkwardness of an independent Nigerian government expelling a missionary group, the church elders believed an orderly trans-

† In those days a person usually had one name and added the name of his town for further identification. Today we use a family name, which one gets from the father.

fer would help. But the actual takeover was rushed, unceremonial, and done with little fanfare. I was happy when it happened because I knew how strong was Nigeria's anti-South Africa feeling. (Later, when I became Nigeria's Minister of Health, Nigeria's antagonism towards South Africa was so great we investigated alternative sources for a snake-bite serum that South Africa usually supplied. We found some in Europe).

When the matter was being discussed between the Americans and the Dutch, we Christians asked the CRC missionaries to accept the DRCM operation if it were offered. We too believed that independence was coming.

Yes, the church was growing rapidly at the time. The same was true for Islam. Unfortunately, we Christians failed to grasp the significance of its growth. With it grew the idea that Christianity was a "foreign religion" and Islam was Nigeria's religion.

The transfer of DRCM to CRC presented a splendid challenge to Christian Reformed missionaries and new Christians to expand the areas in which the Good News was being told. It was of the Lord. Things happened. Some CRC missionaries moved to Tiv compounds. Many additional buildings were required: Harga, Mkar, Zaki Biam and more. It was great work, and we were part of it. Beside serving the Jukun people from the Benue-Takum-Wukari-Baissa region, the CRC Mission now included the entire Tiv area from Makurdi to Zaki Biam, Katsina Ala, and Harga.

We anticipated an expanded church — the Tiv and the Jukun together — one body united in Jesus Christ.

But disappointment crept in. Our Tiv brothers and sisters were used to their separate existence under the Dutch Reformed Church, and the Tiv church was larger than the Benue church. Also, the Tiv and Jukun differ culturally from each other. The Benue Church was rather happy that the Mission headquarters happened to be in our area, but the Tiv were not. When the Nigerian church became indigenous, misunderstanding cropped up when our Tiv brothers and sisters decided to maintain their independence separately from the Benue Church. They organized a separate denomination, the "Nongue Kristu Sudan hen Tiv" (NKST), autonomous from the Benue churches.

The Benue Church then had no option. It had sprung outward from Lupwe, and in 1957 organized itself as a separate denomination, "The Christian Reformed Church of Nigeria" (CRCN). Tribal divisiveness continued even further, and before long the Kutep tribe broke away from what they regarded as Jukun domination. It became "Eklisiyar Kristi a Sudan" (EKAN).

I deplore these divisions; they are so wrong. They sadden me. All of my life I have seen how the ignoring of our equality and unity in Jesus Christ has affected us adversely in social, economic, educational, and religious contexts. Independent, individual, self-governing churches that have no reason for separate existence other than tribal loyalties trouble me greatly.

As a Nigerian Christian I came to know Jesus Christ through the words and works of missionaries, for which I thank my God. But, I deplore the role of those who failed to openly teach and admonish Christians that the Body of Jesus Christ has no space for tribalism. They should have urged and worked for tribal-blind unity in Jesus and in his church. From their own history of the church, they knew the tragedy of division: the breaking away of the Anglicans from Rome, the secession of the Methodists, the breaking up of denominations both in Europe and the United States and on and on. Besides, they were the ones who had taught Nigerians the principle of Christ's united body! Their influence might well have prevailed in the new Nigerian church.

However, one leaves this delicate matter in the hands of Almighty God who created humankind from the earth's dust. The only consolation I have is that the division has not silenced the Good News. God is still speaking; people in Nigeria are still meeting his Son, our Savior Jesus. And, in the Christian Association of Nigeria — in whose services I have spent many of both my early and late years — we recognize that we are truly of one family, the same family, in Jesus Christ.

11

Birth of a Nation

Yes, it was a momentous decade, the decade of the '50s, for the Mission and for the country. Nor did my life remain untouched. The work and focus of the CRC Mission changed remarkably. The number of Christians grew and the reaching out continued. Our small technical school at Lupwe began to yield positive results.

Its first three students, bright and eager young men — Yusuf, Sabo, and Gambo — became outstanding builders — even though we teachers taught in Hausa from an English geometry textbook. Not only did they serve the Mission well but also, to my delight, they helped me construct my first modern house, the foundation of which we laid on Nov. 28, 1949.

The Mission needed more skilled workmen, so training became increasingly important to the Mission's rapid expansion. Evangelism grew steadily in Fikyu, Bissaula, Bete and other surrounding villages. In May 1952, Rev. Smith, Ray Grissen, Rev. Peter Ipema (a missionary stationed at Zaki Biam), and I went to Toro-Dongo to select a site for a mission there. We selected a site at Harga where later a Bible school also was established. Meanwhile, we began construction in Baissa and added buildings at Zaki Biam, Mkar, and Wukari.

The Christian Reformed Mission (and many other mission groups in Nigeria) established several Christian schools. Many, if not most, of the students (including the Hausa and Fulani) who went to Mission schools became Christians. As these Christians spread out, they spread the Good News of Jesus throughout the North. Today Christian school graduates are the salt of our nation.

What a glorious, challenging time for me! And then it happened!

The event that most saddened me also challenged me. Rev. Smith requested that I take over the Mission building department in January 1954. The occasion, however, filled me with grief. Ray Grissen, his wife and four little children returned to the States due to the illness of his wife. He and I had become dear Christian friends during the nearly two short years we had worked together.

After Ray left, my duties increased greatly. So did the pressure. I rarely spent a day at home. I disliked especially the added duty of purchasing equipment, building materials and supplies — which Ray had done until now — and the responsibility of handling the money involved.

I was acutely aware that I was the first black man entrusted by the white man with so much responsibility — and money. By the grace of God and prudent practice, I managed my assignment successfully. I was happy that my work could be seen as a credit to my people.

I thought increasingly about my country and its future. A quiet but exciting sense of approaching freedom from white man's colonialism was growing among us. Independence was in the air. I was optimistic. Freedom. Finally. Too long had we been ruled by the British. At times a deep-seated restlessness surfaced or intensified, especially among leaders who were concerned about the future of Nigeria.

Although a 20th-century history can provide the reader with a complete background of British imperialism in Nigeria, a very brief comment about Nigeria's history will help the reader better understand our country's situation today.

In 1914 the British amalgamated several areas roughly known as Nigeria, and in which they had commercial interests. Further changes in its borders were outlined in the "Berlin divisions of Africa" after World War I.

Before 1914, part of the Sudanic belt, which Nigeria now occupies, was essentially a story of migration and fusion of people, rise and fall of empires, slave trade and its later replacement by trade in tropical produce (bene seeds, soya beans, groundnuts, cotton, and more). The English first established colonialism in areas profitable to trade. Gradually England expanded its rule to both north and south, which control continued until the birth of independent Nigeria in 1960.

As a protectorate of Great Britain, Nigeria was placed under a unitary administration presided over by a Governor-General. For administrative convenience the British divided the country into four parts: the Northern, Eastern, and Western Provinces, and the colony of Lagos. (My home town, Takum, I am told, was part of former Northern Nigeria.)

The 1922 Constitution had introduced "direct election" of representatives in a Council that served as advisor to the British. The Council had no legislative power. Direct election was extremely limited, however; only Lagos and Calabar in Southern Nigeria enjoyed the privilege. (These two towns had been created by the British Lord Frederick Lugard.) Nevertheless, creation of the advisory council and direct election in Lagos and Calabar were a significant response to the political agitation of the Nigerian elites (including Herbert Macaulay, Dr. Nnamdi Azikiwe, and others), who much preferred to elect their own representatives rather than having the British hand-pick them.

In 1946 the British gave the then-existing provinces the responsibility of advising the central government on matters affecting the provinces. In 1951, under a new constitution, the Regional Administration in each province became the Regional Government. That was an important development.

As a Christian concerned about the welfare of Nigeria, my interest in politics and government grew steadily. The country now consisted of three regions: Northern, Eastern, and Western. Each region had its own House of Assembly, and the central government, through its Parliament, had responsibility for finance, defense, and external affairs. Each region could make its own laws, providing they did not conflict with the laws of the federal government.

In 1956 I became the first elected member to the Northern House of Assembly for Wukari. It was not difficult to defeat my opponent, a Northern People's Congress (NPC) candidate. He was supported mainly by the

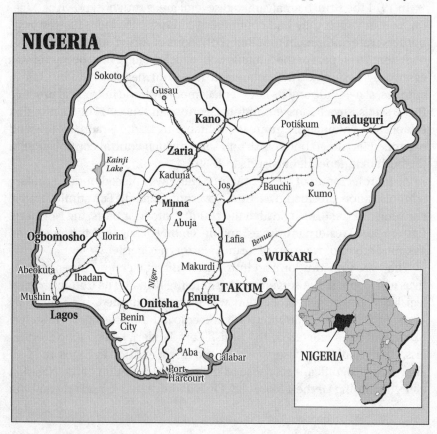

neo-colonialists, the Hausa-Fulani caucus. I contested as an independent candidate.

My first test in the House of Assembly faced me almost immediately. The concerns I had long felt and pondered over now faced me directly. I challenged the Speaker of the House of Assembly for allowing only Muslim prayers to be said at the opening of a session. Nigeria after all, I maintained, was pluralistic. Christians and traditionalists comprised the majority. I argued that governmental power and authority would be abused if it were used to compel non-Muslim citizens to accept a religion that they could not accept. I commented that the Speaker himself and Premier Sir Ahmadu Bello had pledged emphatically that the Christian religion would in no way be interfered with after self-government and independence were declared. Now he was ignoring his own position.

Muslim leaders, I knew, regarded Christian missionaries as the personification of Satan and the British as great imperialists. But, should Islam be imposed upon the non-Muslim population in the North? I knew that without the moral and financial support of the government, the forcing of Islam in the North would not be tolerated.

As a result of my protest, both Christian and Islamic prayers were said before and after the business of the House. It also paved the way for Christian members of the House to exchange ideas on some of the problems that would face Christianity when our independence became reality. Even though a few Christian members identified themselves with the NPC, we shared the same views and aspirations. The influence of Christianity and the church on society was as strong then as it is today. Most of the elected members from Nigeria's Middle Belt Congress (a political party) could not have won without the support of the Christians and the Church.

In 1957 Britain granted the Eastern and Western regions self-government. Lagos became the nation's capital, and Calabar became part of the Eastern Region. The Northern Region, led by Sir Ahmadu Bello, Sardauna of Sokoto, one of Nigeria's most powerful and intelligent leaders, did not accept self-government until March 1959. It needed this time, said Sir Bello, to train people for government positions.

With the turn of the decade, Oct. 1, 1960, Nigeria was born. independence at last! But the influence from Westminster remained the same.

The die had been cast.

What did the future hold?

The Fledgling Politician

The replacement of British officials by Nigerians did not happen all at once. Slowly and cautiously London had moved Nigeria towards independence. The ceremonial office of "Governor-General" did not remain in place too long.

As vice-president of the Northern People's Congress, Sir Abubakar Tofawa Balewa became the first prime minister of Nigeria. Sir Ahmadu Bello, Sardauna of Sokoto, remained the first premier of Northern Nigeria.

Although I had been "elected" to the Northern House of Assembly, it was really through "indirect election." In 1956 Northern Nigeria did not yet vote directly for its representatives. Rather, British colonialists allowed tribal chiefs and other influential Nigerians to hand-pick men (about 100) of demonstrated or potential leadership ability. A limited number of people then were allowed to select from this group one person to represent

Wearing typical native garb, Jolly Tanko Yusuf stands among the members of the Northern House of Assembly in December 1957.

their area. Thus I was chosen to represent Wukari in the Northern House of Assembly.

That system did not continue long, and in 1958 I was re-elected directly by the people. I appreciated being re-elected; it meant I could continue with my task as Deputy Minister of Trade and Industry to which I had been appointed in 1957 by the British Governor of the Northern Region of Nigeria. In 1959 I was transferred to the Ministry of Health and was elevated to acting Minister in 1962. During that time I served as a delegate to the 1962 World Health Organization conference in Geneva, Switzerland.

How exciting to be alive at the time our country was declared independent. I felt particularly fortunate to be involved in politics during a time when the work of many devoted Nigerian leaders in the Middle Belt area was beginning to show results: some dirt roads were tarred, new dirt roads were made, schools were built, and water was made available in some towns. The government hired and appointed people fairly for civil service. It used well the education and training of gifted people. Our leaders tried, quite honestly I believe, to place social justice for all above economic welfare and privileges for some. I was happy, optimistic about the present and future of my country.

Yes, our government's early goals were good. Of course, there was some discrimination, but it wasn't nearly as blatant as it would become in the late 1970s when Nigeria's welfare fell into the hands of military despots. Under its first elected leaders, Nigeria began to build a society that enhanced the well-being of its people.

In 1962 Premier Bello inaugurated the ministerial post of Provincial Commissioner, a position for which only elected representatives were eligible. This new post replaced the British Provincial Resident (who then became the Provincial Secretary.) Up to this time I was a Deputy Minister (known as Parliamentary Secretary) in the House of Assembly,

Jolly Tanko Yusuf in 1957.

but Premier Bello then honored me with an appointment to the new position as Provincial Commissioner.

At 39, I was very young for this position. My experience as a government official was limited. Only since 1957 had I been involved in active governmental politics. To receive this appointment was indeed an honor. I accepted it with some awe and a sharp sense of my responsibility as a Christian governmental servant. I believed God was particularly calling — and challenging — me to witness for him politically.

One would think that a Provincial Commissioner could serve best among his own people. However, the Premier thought it better that Provincial Commissioners not serve in their own province. This meant I would not have to face the rioting that was continually erupting among the Tiv people in my home state, Benue.

I was wrong.

Sir Bello sent me to Benue. No other Provincial Commissioner wanted to be posted in my state, a hotbed of civil unrest! I was the only commissioner sent to his own province. Arson, killing, rioting, rape, and extensive vandalism in Benue had created havoc, suffering, and fear. The British Provincial Resident had not succeeded in establishing peace, and it became my task to quell the riots.

The fighting Tiv created more than enough problems for a young Nigerian, a fledgling politician, in a very young country. It required not merely courage to face such an unpredictable situation but more importantly the support of the Tiv people. I soon learned I had a good supply of this commodity!

Three factors deepened the simmering unrest: First, the census of 1963, taken shortly after I accepted the position, was considered unfair. The Tiv felt they had been undercounted. Second, the frequent encroachment of fertile Tiv farmland by people from the eastern provinces was resented. And third, any domination by the Hausa/Fulani tribes was detested.

When I was assigned to this post, I immediately set about reading any and all the British reports on file, and I investigated every part of the controversy.

I soon discovered and understood why the Tiv people were divided, fighting and killing one another. I concluded that the 1963 census could very easily have been mishandled and the final count affected. Census-taking in Nigeria was a bit haphazard to say the least. Some small areas, particularly in the north, were completely overlooked.

Usually the government appointed people to go to various towns or specified places to count heads. These census takers asked the leaders of the village to get the people out of their huts to be counted physically. If a person said he had 10 children, the counter would ask, "Where are they?

You must show them." This wasn't always done, and it was not difficult for errors to creep in.

In some places the census takers themselves inflated the figures. In others, they failed to count everyone. In addition, some families brought their daughters for counting but not their sons. Although parents usually preferred sons and were proud of them, their presence at the time of the census meant higher taxes. Females, on the other hand, were not assessed. I noted, as I checked further into census counts, that some boys from my own family in Takum had not been counted.

An accurate census is so important. Since Nigeria's independence, all the efforts of governments to obtain an accurate census have failed. Religio-political considerations have led to population manipulation. Muslims need a "majority" to justify their political decisions and religious advances. Due to pressure from Islamic fundamentalists, no government has had the will to count heads honestly and accurately. In view of this reluctance, the nation has always depended on the 1963 census, which was also forged along religious lines — at least in Benue and some other northern states.

At this time Benue Province was twice as large as it is today. It was soon obvious to me that indeed the Tiv had legitimate complaints. In addition to the questionable census count, there also had been discrimination in development, improvements, appointments, and more. Much of the Tiv fighting was politically motivated. Three major political parties were involved: The Northern People's Congress (NPC), led by the Sardauna of Sokoto, the National Council of Nigeria and Cameroon (NCNC), led by Dr. Namdi Azikiwe and the Action Group (AG), led by Chief Abufomi Awolowo. Other smaller parties were only marginally involved.

The second major Tiv problem was land encroachment. Borders and boundaries are mostly traditional, but sometimes they are revised — for good reason — or no reason. Disputes and arguments arose in Benue from time to time, and frequent fighting broke out. For example, a man might live in Benue, with a river providing the border to his land. People who lived on the other side of the river, even though they had fertile soil, could see land on the Benue side, equally fertile, so they "crossed over." People on the Benue side, of course, didn't appreciate encroachment. Small wonder! They needed this land themselves, and others, not even of Benue, were taking it. Part of the problem was that some segments of the area lie in the northern and other in the eastern region of Niger River. Geography encouraged two regions. The encroachers met fierce resistance; fighting and killing were frequent. On more than one occasion I went with the police to settle a particularly nasty dispute. Or, I would go with elders of the church, district officers, and provincial commissioners from both sides to mediate the argument by determining legitimate boundaries. If necessary new boundaries were set.

My task in Benue was far from easy. Many people doubted that I could handle one of the largest states in the northern part of the country. Even though I am a Jukun and not a Tiv, I went ahead in faith. It helped that I understood the Tiv people; we had many of them in my area. I understood their culture, which I respect highly, and I also understood some of their language. I liked them — they are likeable by nature. I had no secret political agenda; I wanted only to help them. I had been taught from childhood that every human being is a human being in the eyes of God. I saw people as they were — some good, some not so good — and I accepted them all. I could embrace them as one of my own. And more importantly, I believed that because God had placed me here, he would also help me. He did.

Gradually the people, especially the Tiv Christians, realized that I wanted to help them solve their problems, not to increase them. They could see that as a Christian I understood that, indeed, they were being discriminated against. Sometimes I held private discussions with the church elders. A Tiv pastor, Rev. Sai, was particularly helpful. He accepted me as a son and I went to him for advice and guidance frequently.

Nevertheless, the situation remained tense. Explosive.

Some Tiv rioters, aided by some disgruntled soldiers from Enugu focused their anger on me. Certain soldiers who supported the govern-

As Provincial Commissioner in charge of Benue State, Yusuf sits astride a horse presented to him in 1963 by the chief of Keffi, during one of his official tours of Benue Province. (Yusuf returned the horse.)

ment kept me informed. The unit attacked Takum, my home town. Not only that, but also they manipulated the arrest of the Chief of Takum, his Highness Alhaji Ali Ibrahim, and several of his councilors whom they took to Wukari.

The Chief of Takum was arrested "on suspicion" that the government of Sardauna might have sent weapons through me to defend Takum. But it was not the Army itself that invaded the town. It was a small group of disgruntled soldiers encouraged by some of the Tiv living around the borders of Takum and Gboko who wanted to take over Takum. Politically inspired, they wanted to fight and extend their territory.

I had encouraged the soldiers not to extend the rioting to the Wukari section because the people in that area were largely peaceful. Rumors had spread that I would send an army to Takum to stop the fighting (which I would not have done). So, to embarrass me, they took the chief of my home town to Wukari! There the late Aku Uka, his Highness Mallam Adi Byewe, and District Officer Mallam Yeldu tried unsuccessfully to persuade the Army to release Chief Alhaji Ali Ibrahim. Consequently Mallam Yeldu and Mallam Yerima Enoch Audu Ibrahim, the Takum Chief's brother, drove to Makurdi to report the incident to me.

I summoned a meeting of the Security Committee, comprised of the police commissioner, the battalion Commanding Officer Major Aba Kyari, the Provincial Secretary, and a police commissioner, and myself. We deliberated.

Meanwhile I acted. This kind of nonsense I simply would not tolerate. I prepared to go to Wukari myself. If the chief of my own home town and his councilors were not released, then I would go to jail with him. The Security Committee was appalled at my decision and tried to prevent my going.

"I am not bluffing," I told them. "If I am to remain here, you will send a wireless to the unit Commanding Officer of the soldiers involved. He must order the immediate release of the Chief of Takum and his councilors and their return to Takum."

The silence was intense. After several minutes the Security Committee agreed.

I did not go to Wukari. Major Kyari received word that night that the Commanding Officer at Wukari had released the chief and his councilors and had taken them back to Takum. The people were surprised that I had taken no revenge.

The crisis, at least for now, was over.

Serious questions still remained. Terrorism and fighting continued. My heart was heavy. I was burdened with the violence; I detest it with all my being. Yet when the rioters burned houses and killed people, no matter how I felt, I had to be courageous. I tried. At times I went with the police and the Provincial Secretary to talk with rioters. We interrogated many of them, but after a few days we ordered most of them released. When the Honorable J.S. Tarka, leader of the United Middle Belt Congress, was arrested, I instructed the authorities that he be granted bail. The authorities reported to the Premier that I was interfering with their work, but the government accepted my position.

I looked at what to me seemed like a puzzle that existed among the Tiv. Really there were two people, twins, you might say — the Bapuso (Cain) and the Bachogo (Abel) elements of the tribe. The ruling Tiv chief, a Christian, at this time was from the Bachogo. He was the first to acknowledge and accept my mission. He agreed that the Tiv should not fight among themselves simply because J. S. Tarka came from the Bapuso. J.S. Tarka was a Tiv leader; he resisted the political domination of the Fulani-Hausa. The Tiv people wanted their own state.

I also visited J.S. Tarka's father to show my respect for his having come to my residence in Makurdi and to talk peace with him. He promised to help stop the fighting and did his best. To prove to the people that Tarka's father was on my side, we sat down together in places where the people could see us together.

I also enjoyed the support of the district officers, the police commissioner and the security agents.

But always I felt sadness. Deep sadness. I turned to my God often. I said, "Here I am, God, in your hands. You created this people. You placed me here. Help me now to know how to stop and settle this violence." Any courage I had, I had from God; he brought me through. Misunderstandings could have arisen so easily, because here I was, a Jukun trying to solve Tiv problems. Sometimes, for security or political reasons the people even blamed me, but generally the Christian community of Tiv land realized that I was not tribalistic, for I had no reason to be. Simply, I loved the Tiv.

The suffering cut deeply. Property damage was widespread. I advised victims to rebuild their houses quickly. I told them if they could build their houses within a week or two, the government would give them money for rebuilding. Sometimes I personally helped them; I carried water from the tanks and gave food to people who had lost everything. I prayed and I called for prayers of the church leaders and Christians.

Fortunately for me, the majority of the Tiv were Christians. Church leaders provided opportunities for me to explain my mission to the people and to ask them, as Christian to Christians, to help stop the rioting. "Why do we kill our own?" I asked. Again I appealed to Jesus' prayer (John 17:20-25) for Christians living together on this earth:

My prayer is not for them alone. I pray also for those who will believe in me through their message, that all of them may be one, Father, just as you are in me and I am in you. May they also be in us so that the world may believe that you have sent me. I have given them the glory that you gave me, that they may be one as we are one: I in them and you in me. May they be brought to complete unity to let the world know that you sent me and have loved them, even as you have loved me.

Father, I want those you have given me to be with me where I am, and to see my glory, the glory you have given me because you loved me before the creation of the world.

Righteous Father, though the world does not know you, I know you, and they know that you have sent me. I have made you known to them, and will continue to make you known in order that the love you have for me may be in them and that I myself may be in them.

I asked, "If we are one with Christ and with each other, then how can we kill each other?"

By the grace of God, first of all, and by support of the mainly peace-loving Tiv people, the situation improved, even stopped after the 1964 election. Once again God had demonstrated to me that unity is necessary if a nation wants to maintain internal peace.

With the Benue state having returned to peace, it seemed too that my work there was finished. I was transferred to Zaria, and I wondered what awaited me there.

A Growing Family

God had blessed my family with several children, seven of them, by my first wife, Matan Fara Kunga. For personal medical reasons discovered by her doctor, it was no longer possible for us to live together.

God said, "It is not good for the man to be alone. I will make a helper suitable for him." (Ge. 2:18) With seven young children and a very heavy work load, I could think of no alternative other than to seek a wife of my choice. I needed a wife, of course, who would willingly help me bring up my seven children — no small responsibility or task, I realized. Times were changing. Today differed greatly from the days of my childhood when relatives cared deeply for one another and even helped to raise one another's children.

After searching diligently I found Massey Fashanu, who agreed to mother my children. We married. But when our daughter Sarah was born, I learned, to my sorrow, that Massey did not want Sarah to be the sister of my other children and live together with them. She wanted Sarah to be her child alone and not one among many children. This hurt me; it was not easy to accept Massey's decision.

Adding to the complexity of

Sarah Tanko Yusuf was the daughter of Jolly Tanko Yusuf and his second wife, Massey Fashanu.

my life at this time was my appointment as Agent-General to the United Kingdom for the Northern Region of Nigeria in September 1965. As an agent-general my task was to represent to the British the commercial and cultural interests of Northern Nigeria. Accepting this appointment meant that I and my family would have to move to London.

This did not suit Massey. She refused to go to England with me. She said she would come "some time later" and bring Sarah along. But I needed her now. Transferring to a foreign country was not only new for me, but also it might be very difficult for some of my children, ages 5 to 12 years.

Nor did Massey come to England later. A nursing sister, she decided that her work was more important than coming to England with me and caring for the children.

Accepting the appointment to England was not without other personal pain to me as well. I felt particularly fortunate that I was involved in politics at a time when the work of many devoted Nigerian leaders in the Wukari Division and the Middle Belt was bearing fruit. The government was distributing amenities among its people fairly. It hired and appointed people fairly for civil service. It used well the scholarship of gifted people. The leaders tried, quite honestly, to place social justice above economic welfare and peace.

Accepting this appointment would mean that I and my children would have to leave our beloved country. I found it hard to quit the field of active elective politics, a field where I had been happy. I had made many friends, not only within my tribe but also throughout the country. I weighed the pros and cons of my appointment carefully: my duties as a servant of God, work, my family, tribe, political party, and my country. Eventually I realized that such opportunities are not often offered more than once in a lifetime, especially to Christians. I should accept, with gratitude.

I accepted — with gratitude.

My children and I traveled to England in September 1965, together yet alone. We missed family — uncles, aunts, cousins, and friends. I felt I had left part of myself behind, but I would never forget the people of my region. From my office in Zaria I wrote a farewell letter to the people of my Wukari Division (see Appendix), which contained many of my ideas about the need for moral politics based on unity. Party leaders and others read my letter at NPC party meetings in many villages throughout Wukari Division.

My ideas on unity were being disseminated. I was grateful. I left Wukari with peace.

My children and I arrived in England, and set ourselves immediately to finding proper schools. At great expense, I put the children in appropriate boarding schools. Only after I had settled them into the routine of boarding school, could I devote my attention to my new assignment.

My task in England was short-lived.

On Jan. 15, 1966, there was a coup in Nigeria. The British Broadcasting Company and the local daily newspapers blared the news — Nigeria's government overthrown! A military coup. I grieved for my country, and in a more personal way, realized that my family's small world was also topsy-turvy again! Myriads of thoughts went through our minds and our conversation became serious. We had been in England three months.

I was not really surprised, however. During my service in Benue the behavior of the army, which was under the command of Gen. Jan Ironsi and the first division of the army based in Kaduna, made me think there would be a coup.

For a week, or two, or three I heard nothing. I felt as if I were treading nowhere — keeping busy, going no place, and setting no goals. The new president was Gen. Ironsi. The more I heard about the military victory and

As Agricultural Minister of Health, Northern Nigeria, Jolly Tanko Yusuf turns to converse with others at the 1962 World Health Organization conference in Geneva, Switzerland.

the circumstances of the coup the more I realized we were in trouble. His rule would be unstable, perhaps followed soon by another coup.

We were at a small reception in honor of the senior officers who had been sent to close the Nigerian Agent General offices when we learned that we were sacked. It was the end of February 1966, and Gen. Ironsi abolished all four Nigerian Agent General positions in the United Kingdom. My work in England was finished before it really began.

Now what? I had no reason to stay in England. But what about my children? They had barely settled. How could I uproot them again?

In March an officer from the Ministry of External Affairs arrived in London. "Pack your files and materials," he ordered, "and send them back." I did.

I talked with my children. All of us were upset. Six stayed in school, but Abigail, 7, refused to stay in a foreign country without her father. She and I returned to Nigeria, where she could stay with relatives.

We arrived in April. Before I had gone to England, Premier Sir Bello had bought my car, but he had not paid me for it. So that I would lose no money in accepting the assignment to England, he had agreed to purchase it as one of the conditions of my acceptance of the appointment. When I returned I needed my car and began to look for it because things had changed with the coup. I found it near a mosque, locked in a garage. The back glass was shattered — perhaps from the path of the bullet that had killed the premier.

Before I had opportunity to use it however, the government placed me under house arrest at 22 Lafia Road in Kaduna. Armed soldiers guarded me. They provided my ordinary daily needs, and a cook and a steward attended me.

I tried to get my attendants to contact the government to request the governor to see me. Finally, two weeks later, upon seeing Lt. Col. Hassam Katsina, the military governor of Northern Nigeria, I requested permission to go to Takum to see my aged mother, who I knew would be anxious about my fate after the coup. Within two days he released me, having obtained permission from the new president, Gen. Ironsi.

"Why have I been detained?" I asked.

He told me the new leader suspected that because of my former governmental activities as Minister of Health and as Provincial Commissioner, I might become involved in initiating a counter coup.

I smiled. I said, "Do you really think I would stage a counter coup? Could I stage a counter coup without a gun in my hands?"

With that our discussion ended.

I left soon for Takum and spent a night in Makurdi where I received a wireless from the military governor's office inviting me to return to

Kaduna to attend a conference of Northern Nigeria's so-called Leaders of Thought (a government-selected group of opinion-makers and thought-changers from various parts of the country). I and J. S. Tarka, who was then on the opposing side, were to represent Benue. The agenda included discussion and possible decision concerning the future of Nigeria.

Having traveled this far to see Mother, I quickly traveled to Takum to spend a day with her. I briefed her on what had happened to her son and her grandchildren, and then I returned to Kaduna.

During the meeting a few Northern Nigerians, including me, were selected to work together with other Leaders of Thought from the east, west, and midwest sections of the country. We discussed whether Nigeria should be a federation, a confederation, or whether it should break away totally.

After a few days of meetings, I observed that Lt. Col. Ojuku, who was the military governor of Eastern Nigeria, had refused to send delegates to attend the meetings. We waited and waited. In vain. I sensed that a crisis in the country would lead to another coup or secession. My suspicion was based on the assassinations of Sir Ahmadu Bello and Mallam Abubakar Tafawa Balewe, who were killed Jan. 15, 1966.

The next blow came soon. On July 29, 1966, Gen. Ironsi's regime was toppled when Northern military men staged a counter coup. It didn't surprise me. In addition, this coup was initiated by young officers from the Northern part of the country. Because of the poor or non-existent communication among the three regions in Eastern Nigeria, Biafra in fact did try to break away in 1967. Its unsuccessful attempt ended in 1970 when Federal government troops defeated the Biafrans.

Since I was no longer under a cloud with the government, I thought about working for it again. I did not want my diploma in public administration and my experience to lie idle. I wanted to serve somehow, preferably my country. I applied to the Federal Public Service Commission, the board that employed staff for federal institutions and agencies. It offered me three positions: Ambassador to Guinea, Consul General to New York, or Consul General to Germany.

I thought of my children. None of the three appointments would take me back to England. The rank of Ambassador was higher than that of Consul General, but Germany would station me nearer to my children in England. I accepted that position. Joseph, Christiana, Ruth and Deborah remained in their schools in England. Eventually I found good international schools in Germany for my younger children, Fatima and Rakiya in Germany, so I moved them to Hamburg.

Here I learned positively that Massey had no intention of joining me. She refused to come with Sarah to Germany. Our marriage was over. What remained was the negotiation of the legal aspects, including custody of lit-tle Sarah. Massey refused my request. She wanted Sarah.

What should I do? What could I do? I could not face extended litigation over Sarah at this difficult time. My decision not to fight for Sarah was very, very difficult, but no one could predict the outcome of a legal battle at a time when the very future of our country was in doubt. After considering all the ramifications, I had no alternative other than to unwillingly give in to Massey's demand.

The coup and its aftermath shook the foundation of our young coun-try. The evidence of our nation's instability and continuing crisis lay in the names of soldiers and people brutally killed. Christians were used to kill Christians. It grieved me even more that almost all of the casualties were from northern and eastern Nigeria, and the Middle Belt. I saw the insta-bility of the government. I realized then, with a deep sense of anxiety, another coup would follow, and after that perhaps a counter coup, to be followed by what? I did not know. Again I realized we had to do something about tolerance and unity, and Christians would have to show the way. We had Jesus Christ, the only real foundation for accepting one another as brothers and sisters, images of God.

Comfort Tanko Yusuf carries Rakiya while Deborah and Fatima stand beside her.

Would there be no end? Even though I was now in Germany, my heart was so heavy, and at times sadness overwhelmed me. Still I found comfort; I knew God controlled the world, including Nigeria, including my family. I continued working, of course, but sadly.

I also resumed my search for a wife to share my life and to help me with my children. Again God answered my prayers. I found her in West Germany in 1967. Comfort Okojie, a Nigerian lady, had come to West Germany for education and training in home economics, specializing in hotel management. I was delighted to meet Comfort (a lovely and appropriate name for her). I was happy when she agreed to become my wife and the mother to my children — if her parents consented.

We returned to Nigeria together. After becoming acquainted with Comfort's parents and sharing with them information about myself and my children, I asked her parents' consent to the marriage. They agreed. I paid an appropriate dowry and greeted her parents, immediate family, and others connected with the family. We married in 1969 according to native law and customs of Benin in Midwestern Nigeria.

Again I experienced God's personal concern for me and my family. I appreciate deeply Comfort's devoted love and affection. We had two sons together, David and Ibrahim, but Comfort gave her love not only to me and the two boys but also to all of our children.

I am short of adequate words to express my gratitude to God for his blessings. The Lord before whom I walk not only sent me 10 children, but also he cares for them. I thought of the deaths of many members — many still young — of Grandfather Aluku's family, starting from Grandfather himself. I looked at Comfort's and my family — all in good health.

My cup overflows. I thank my Jesus.

Islam Explained

Since Nigeria's independence, the problem that has challenged me and has taken much of my concern and prayer, has been Nigeria's momentum toward Islamization. Discrimination comes in many forms. Discriminatory actions are often based on census reports, election results, and other statistics based on tribal membership and religious ties. Small wonder these numbers have always been disputed.

Why is there such conflict between Muslims and Christians? A close look at Islam, and especially a comparison of it with Christianity, will help the reader see why vigilance and action are constantly required.

Islam began in the year 622 A.D., some six centuries after Jesus Christ was born. Four decades later Islam's disciples had already gained control, mainly by sword, of Northern Africa. By 1050 the rulers of the large medieval kingdoms of Mali and Songhai in West Africa had been "converted" to Islam. Its message soon spread to Nigeria.

In Islamic countries — such as Saudi Arabia and Kuwait and other Middle East countries — religion and government are one and the same. There it is considered legitimate for Muslim political leaders to use state facilities, institutions, and power to promote Islam. It seemed natural then, when Nigerian self-government began in 1956 and up to 1959, to Muslim leaders that they openly use government for both religious and political purposes.

Muslims believe that Allah, through the Qu'ran (Koran), has given only to them his final revelation and instructions. Further, Allah has called them to enforce his will and word as explained in the Qu'ran. For all fundamentalist Muslims — young and old, moderate or zealot — Islam carries the harsh, intolerant and fanatical imperative to convert or conquer by force all "other children" of Allah — whom Muslims regard as unbelievers. Belief in an Allah interpreted any other way than Islam's Allah will not erase (for the Muslim) the label "infidel" or "unbeliever" for that person.

Christians too believe that God has revealed himself in his Word, the holy Bible. Christians too seek to follow the precepts expressed in God's Word. Christians too desire that others believe in Jesus Christ as Savior. But God's love, not force, is the compelling power. Belief in Jesus Christ, the Son of Almighty God, cannot be coerced by humankind but must be inspired by God through his Word.

A country like Nigeria, whose 300 tribes approach religion in so many different ways, requires a government that recognizes each human being as a person who can and must make religious and spiritual decisions for himself or herself. It is this deep conviction about God and his Son Jesus Christ that fuels my concern for individual rights and freedom and compels my total effort for my people.

As far as fundamentalist Muslims are concerned, three alternatives exist for dealing with unbelievers. First, infidels must be converted. Second, if not converted, they must be subjugated. Third, if they are neither converted nor subjugated, they must be eliminated.

To Islamic fundamentalists all non-Islamic religions are both heretical and hopeless. They tolerate no viewpoint other than their own. Islamic law and religion must be accepted — if not willingly then by force. It must by the way of life of all citizens.

Unbelievers include all non-Muslims. Islam's task is everywhere and forever. Infidels are to be humiliated; denied due process of law, employment in key places, and social justice; and ultimately killed if they refuse to convert to Islam. Such actions are justified in the Sunnah, which contains all the teachings of Islam's greatest prophet, Mohammed. Vindication for this harsh philosophy is found in the fundamentalist's interpretation of Qu'ran 9:29: "Fight against such of those who have been given the Scripture as believers not in Allah nor the Last Day."

At this interpretation, a Christian shudders who believes that "God so loved the world that he gave his only begotten Son, that whosoever believes in him shall have everlasting life." (John 3:16). But such a brutal strategy is what turns fundamentalists into fanatics. It is difficult if not impossible to change their illusion that Islam only possesses the truth about God. Consequently, Nigerian Muslims believe they are God's policemen. If a person dies while enforcing Islamic laws or while burning churches and killing infidels, he will instantly go to paradise as his reward. Hence many fundamentalists do not fear death; they carry out their dangerous missions "in the name of Allah." Only recently has the world witnessed the Iranian revolution, which provoked eight years of war (1976–1984) in the Persian Gulf. It is a tragic example of the radical movement some fanatics want to succeed in Nigeria.

Fundamentalists even regard moderate Muslims, who do not subscribe to this law of the jungle, as infidels deserving of harsh treatment. Not all Muslims are fundamentalists, of course. And moderate Muslims do make some allowance for non-believers: a treaty may be negotiated with infidels that may spare their lives. In that case, however, the infidel becomes a dhimmi, a person marked as an infidel and subject to various restrictions similar to those of South Africa's white apartheid regulations, although this is not common in Nigeria. A dhimmi must wear identifiable clothing and must live in a clearly marked house. He may possess no good thing enjoyed by Muslims and may not bear arms.

It is easy to see then why Muslim fundamentalists have no room for a government neutral to its pluralistic population. In young Nigeria where not only are there Christians and Muslims, but hundreds of tribes that follow the traditional religions handed down to them, neutrality in the government is necessary. Many tribes have followed their religions for centuries.

For Muslims, the Qu'ran prescribes rules for religious, political, and personal life. This is dramatically verified in the Islamic Council's "Model of an Islamic Constitution" submitted by the Council of Ulama (religious experts) to the Constitution Review Committee of Nigeria in 1987. The committee hoped that Nigeria one day would accept this model as the basis for its constitution. Islamic ideology defines a "state" as: "a geographically delineated segment of human society united by common obedience to a single sovereign and referring either to the society as a whole or more specifically to the sovereign authority which exercises both legal and concrete powers."

Some Muslims maintain that the state is "a concrete representation of culture and embodies the basic structure of culture and acts in its behalf." Therefore the state (government) must control and govern the lives of its citizens. Some Muslim scholars have gone even further. They maintain that Sharia requires government to supervise all aspects of Nigerian lives, no matter how trivial these aspects might be to those who do not subscribe to Islam. Included are such matters as mode of dress, relationships, attitude towards work, and the way Muslims enter their houses! Anything contrary to such regulations is tantamount to rejection of an important aspect of Islam. Thus an Islamic government that follows the provisions of the Sharia will govern all aspects of human life.

Nigerian Islamic leaders, even though they be moderate Muslims, have pushed Islam as hard as they could during the more than three decades since our independence. They have maneuvered jurisdiction over religion, education, economic, and personal lives. They have set up Islamic judicial institutions and have instituted administrative policies that aimed to implement Sharia throughout the country.

Even though the behavior of most Muslims is flagrantly at odds with the ideals of Sharia (just as we Christians fall short of the ideals prescribed in God's perfect law), fanatic Muslims keep trying to make Sharia the foundation of law throughout Nigeria. This frightens me greatly.

In its preamble, the Model Constitution states: "... Islam is a complete code of life suitable for all people and all times, and Allah's mandate is universal and eternal and applies to every sphere of human conduct and life." It acknowledges that "the setting up of a society based on Islam and its principles requires the complete application of the Sharia in the constitution and in the law." Someone has said that "Islam is the only monotheistic religion in the world that offers a political system." That political system, the basis for all law, is the Sharia.

On the surface, a reading of the Model Constitution suggests that Muslims do indeed desire a law-abiding citizenry. Article 1 reads: "Sovereignty belongs to Allah alone [as interpreted by Muslims], and the Sharia is paramount." It is comprised of the Qu'ran and the Sunnah (the actions, sayings, and traditions based on the prophet Mohammed), and "is the source of legislation and policy." Further, the Model Constitution (Article 3) says that state and society are based on several principles, the first of which declares "the supremacy of the Sharia and its rules in all walks of life." Stated another way, no laws may be legislated that conflict with Sharia principles. Thus the Sharia is the law. Then, the word "law" as it frequently appears throughout the Model Constitution is a euphemism, a treacherous synonym for Sharia.

Articles in the Model Constitution that are seemingly innocent become false when "law" is read as "Sharia." According to Article 12, "Every person has the right to protection against harassment or victimization by official agencies." At first glance, one would agree that constitutionally employment and employers would make no distinction among applicants based on religion. But, say the Muslims then, Sharia is only for believers. All others are infidels — and I have already explained Islamic instructions regarding infidels.

Article 12 says further, "There is no compulsion in religion." I shake my head.

Article 25 compels all persons in governmental offices on any level — including "the Heads of Armed Forces" to "follow the Sharia in letter and in spirit, to uphold the message of Islam at all costs ...."

Article 42 provides for the establishment of Hisbah — "institutions for supervising and safeguarding the fulfillment of right norms of public behavior. Its purpose is to enforce what is right and forbid what is wrong." Hisbah, according to Article 42, is for "the promotion and protection of Islamic values with a view to establishing what is right and forbidding what is wrong."

Article 57 explains Jihad, known worldwide, which is Islam's religious war. Jihad is every Muslim's "perpetual and inalienable duty" and he must "defend the land of Islam and the Islamic order." Any government not headed by Muslims, then should be brought down by Muslims. To that end, says Article 58, "there shall be a program of Islamic education and training to inculcate in the Armed Forces the concept of Jihad."

Notwithstanding Articles 57 and 58, the Model Constitution also includes both Article 75 which states that "the state is duty bound .... to protect the freedom of man throughout the world," and Article 76 which says, "The State is obligated to refrain from engaging in wars on grounds of difference in religious belief ...." What a despicable contradiction.

That lawmakers may be well aware of the Sharia's effect on pending legislation, Article 65 compels the Council of Ulama to "explain the stand of the Sharia on various legislative proposals" under consideration.

Sharia covers life from peace to war, from private to public, from personal to community, from options to law, from belief to practice. Every situation, from cradle to grave, has been anticipated!

Encounters between Christianity and Islam have never been easy and happy. Muslim fundamentalists see Christians as blasphemers for proclaiming that Jesus Christ is the Son of God — (even though they acknowledge Jesus as one of their prophets). The perplexing question then for Nigeria's 100 million Christians, Muslims, and traditionalists is: can this kind of constitution work in Nigeria?

No!

Christians are not happy with this continual Christian-Muslim tension. But, it will continue until all citizens — Christians, Muslims, and animists — are equal in the eye and in the practice of law and government. Muslim rulers, on the other hand, have despaired the effective voice of Christianity and have denied its rapid growth in Nigeria since independence, especially in the northern parts of the country. Fear has intensified their efforts to Islamize Nigeria.

While Muslims force adherence to the law of Sharia and seek compulsory unity within the family of Islam of all Nigerians, traditionalists and Christians seek a neutral government that permits all its citizens to worship God as they have interpreted him or as they have been taught.

For Christians there is an additional longing — that the unity Jesus Christ demands will be completely ours by choice and conviction so that in our unity, the citizens of Nigeria may see our God of love.

Expansion of Islam

Sometime I ask myself — is Nigeria irrevocably enmeshed in the grip of Islam? If so, how did this happen? Nigeria will not celebrate its 40th birthday until the year 2000. Will my country have a neutral government by then? If God spares my life I will continue to work for a government that recognizes the worth and rights of all its citizens.

Islam, because of its nature, will continue its efforts to impose its will upon the people. Its efforts began before the birth of our country, and it uses any means it can.

Its initial efforts began in Northern Nigeria, the largest of the four regions of Nigeria that together made up the federation from the date of its independence in 1960 until the time of the first military coup in 1966. Its approximately 282,000 square miles occupied three-quarters of the country. These northern states also formed part of a large savanna belt that stretched across Africa, south of the Sahara Desert and north of the equatorial forests.

In fact, the name originally given by the Arab traders to this part of the country was Sudan. Though politically the name was restricted to the large republic formerly known as the Anglo-Egyptian Sudan, movement of peoples along the Sudan belt has been relatively easy and has considerably influenced the history of Nigeria's north. Arab influence, which continues to be felt in Northern Nigeria, began here.

Many Nigerians do not know that before the arrival of the British, Northern Nigeria was culturally and economically oriented not only to Mali and Songhai but also to Egypt and Tripoli. By the end of the 15th century, Islam had already been entrenched as the religion of the citizens of northern towns such as Sokoto, Kano, Katsina, and some parts of Maiduguri and more.

Nigeria's joy in its freedom from colonialism was too soon marred by the zeal of fanatic Muslims to make the country another link in the Islamic chain of nations. Unfortunately, the majority of Nigerians, including Christians, did not recognize Islam's thrust for power and control. Like an octopus Islam grabbed and crushed its opponents, greedily grasping towns and villages wherever it could. These developments troubled me intensely.

Since Nigeria's birthday, three men — Sir Ahmadu Bello, Alhaji Abubakar Gumi, and Gen. Ibrahim Badamasi Babangida — have used their tremendous power to shape Nigeria not only for the age in which they lived but also for an Islamic future.

Sir Ahmadu Bello, Sardauna of Sokoto, a Fulani, was Nigeria's first premier. How could an obscure religious teacher sweep the country, especially the North, with such revolutionary fervor as did he? How did he manage to mutilate Nigeria's constitution so badly? And get away with it? How did he convert Northern Nigeria into an almost theocratic, Islamic state?

Sir Bello once said he would use whatever means necessary to complete the unfinished work of Islamization started by his great grandfather, Shehu Usman dan Fodio, who maintained that "had it not been for the arrival of the Europeans, Islamization would have reached the sea" (in ba don bature be da mun gama da ture). And Sir Bello tried to do just that. He used his political position and power to threaten chiefs and traditional rulers; indirectly he forced weak ones to change to Islam; he bent the law to his own aims; he used district heads and district officers for the same purpose.

Bello's influence on Nigeria was widespread; it was also severely flawed. At his death — this man who would be stripped of his power by a bullet — his mourners and a few intellectuals left the people with many false images. Meanwhile, the rest of Nigerians looked on in stony silence when the coup of January 1966 took place.

Just what was Sir Bello's legacy?

Violent mass emotion inside northern Nigeria is, I think, a realistic enough assessment of the Sardauna's immediate legacy. But this doesn't nearly convey what his leadership meant and how it still affects the areas he ruled. Was he a dedicated prophet bent on returning Nigeria to the old pre-colonial days? Or was he a tyrant who put his own people to the sword and fire and then disappeared, leaving nothing but war widows, high cost of food and bewildered citizens? To read the obituaries you would think that Sir Bello was a phenomenon. A phenomenon he may have been but never the savior of the north that we were asked to believe.

Bello, was not, however, the man who introduced political maneuvering and discrimination against the people of southern Nigeria and Christians in northern Nigeria. The British themselves had developed the strategy of discrimination long before they transferred power to the Muslims in 1960. Yet, Islamization of the government was not a natural extension of the "Nigerianization policy" publicly declared and vigorously pursued by the government at the dawn of Nigeria's independence. Rather, Islamization was merely an historical opportunity! The three-year delay in self-government (postponed from 1956 at Sir Bello's request) and the "Northernization policy" (as Nigerianization had actually become) were deliberate attempts of people in power to prevent Christians from filling vacancies created by expatriates who were leaving the country.

Only astute political observers recognized that by the end of British rule the practice of political and administrative discrimination against Christians, especially in the North, had been fully developed and was being carried out in earnest. In spite of objections and advice to the contrary, political leaders considered it legitimate to use state facilities for the promotion and furtherance of Islam.

Jolly Tanko Yusuf in 1960.

Sir Bello and his aides openly used religion for political purposes. So brazen was his abuse of office that toward the end of his life, Bello spent more time and effort "Islamizing" than as premier of Northern Nigeria and president of the Northern People's Congress. He used government planes, vehicles and other facilities openly and freely for his religious campaigns.

The political philosophy of the Fulani-Hausa Muslims was to develop policies that would entrench "Northern identity and solidarity" in order to prevent fragmentation of the north, which they regarded as their kingdom, and to prevent powerful southern influence. Because this maneuvering and discrimination against the south and against the Christians in the north had been so well-developed before the British handed power to the Muslims, these tactics were considered quite legitimate. Thus, the use of any means, methods, or facilities was merely a good strategy in their plans.

A few courageous members, including myself, strongly criticized this misuse of government facilities. Even though we knew there was not much we could do, we felt we had to speak out as loyal citizens. The Sardauna of Sokoto even set up a secret committee after his return from the Middle East (a solid Islamic bloc) in 1964 to find alternative ways and means of Islamizing the whole North. Thus was born the Jama'atu Nasril Islam (JNI, the people's association).

Nigerian emirs and chiefs, however, hijacked the JNI and replaced the leaders, and other groups, the so-called Izala or Shia groups, were marginalized. This in turn led to the formation of another sect, Jama'atu Izlatu Bidi'a Wa Igamatus Sunna, (Izala) in 1978, with Alhaji Abubakar Gumi as its founder and grand patron.

The majority sect, the Darika, believed the same fundamentals of Islam, but they were less aggressive. Some of them did not welcome Alhaji Gumi and his influence, even though many of the educated Muslims who controlled Izala accepted his leadership. After the death of Sir Bello, some of the Darikans decided to do something about Gumi's power by exercising their influence.

What was the secret of this man Bello who had changed Nigeria so much during its infancy that the wounds of Christians and non-Muslims are today still festering with poverty, pain and misery?

Religious beliefs alone do not explain his authority. Only a few Islamic scholars accepted his claims and his pronouncements. Nor was he a simple fanatic. He tolerated dissent and accepted all sorts of compromises with Christians and the West in the interest of peace as well as in the interest of the government that he was manipulating. Far from manipulating the country and running the entire federation from the confines of a one-story villa in Kaduna, he seems quite literally to have interpreted his role to be the giver of opinion and the guardian of the Islamic faith. During his six years in power, he served as the Sardauna of Sokoto and Kaduna, president of the NPC, Chief Minister, and later on as premier of Northern Nigeria.

His secret was quite simple: Bello focused on his drive for power and maintained his integrity to himself. His smart use of government facilities and privileges, his unrelenting drive and determination — and of course, his use (and abuse) of his power — increased his stature continuously. The root of his fundamentalism lay in his unflagging belief in and loyalty to the Qu'ran. The strength of his vision was its wholeness.

Because he believed firmly that the Qu'ran should guide every Muslim's behavior, it followed that anything that undermined a person's focus on such behavior, things such as western values, the pursuit of money, and more — should be dispensed with. (Of course, the pursuit of money was only bad where it was not used to promote Islam.)

Such absolutism might seem eccentric, if not mad. But it was this "purity" of his Islamic viewpoint that attracted the North where rapid development allowed Bello to carve a holy alliance out of unholy elements: angry students, tribes, a dispossessed peasantry, and the increasing number of restricted women in purdah (men's strict control of women, not allowing them any freedom during the day).

It was a go-ahead for Islam and a setback for Christianity. It created deep unrest among the people. Religious uprisings of national concern had not occurred during British rule, as despite their shortcomings, they made sure that all Nigerians were allowed to hold their religious beliefs.

Sir Ahmadu Bello tried to change all this.

Relationships among various religious groups and government deteriorated after 1960. Under Sir Bello and according to the Islamic point of view, if a town's chief was a Muslim, all citizens under his jurisdiction were regarded — and counted — as Muslims. Not even all the Muslims agreed with Sir Bello's point of view. In 1962-63 religious violence erupted in Argungu (Sokoto state) where riots took many lives. It was a violent sectarian clash among Muslims themselves.

Historically, Muslim conquerors had learned that the best way to control a populace was through religion. Thus, for a conquest to succeed, it was best that the military operation be led by an Islamic religious leader. His assigned strategy was to amass political power both by winning adherents and in controlling the food, shelter, and land. He tried to sustain hordes of adherents and almajirai (students) with food, shelter, and other necessities. Coercion was a method freely used, and helped to spread Islam throughout a conquered area. The objective was to overthrow any religion that did not accept the Qu'ran as the only prescription for life.

Christianity had made deep inroads in Nigeria in the decade of the '50s particularly, and discrimination against young Christians proved to be a powerful tool.

The government used many tactics. It disregarded existing planning laws. It allowed mosques to be built within the proximity of public institutions and churches. Even worse, no sooner had a mosque been built in an area than the Muslim community would object to the continuance of existing churches or Christian establishments.

After the counter coup of 1966, the efforts of Islamic followers became more intense. The military regime of Gen. Yakubu Gowan, which began

after Gen. Ironsi's overthrow, began to take over the Christian schools and
the hospitals. But not without controversy, bitterness, and deep sadness.
The military government refused to reason and used its tentacles to per-
vade every sphere of public life and institutions.

All of this happened during the nine years Gen. Gowan was head of
state, even though — and I am sorry to say this — he was a Christian. During his term of office the Muslim influence increased and he allowed
Christian schools and hospitals to be taken over by the government! Further, during his tenure, government officials reduced — and in some cases
eliminated — the fare for Muslims to make their pilgrimage to Mecca!
Many Christians also took advantage of this gratuity, and insisted that they
be allowed to make a pilgrimage to Jerusalem. Many did!

Some alert Christians watched with dismay. It soon became apparent
that even Christian leaders with power to act often failed to see what was
happening! Can you believe that the earliest efforts to promote Islam with
public funds happened while a Christian occupied the highest position in
Nigeria? (And he had been educated in a Christian school!)

Nor was Islamization restricted to the federal government. State governments also used and still use public funds to establish Islamic schools.
Muslim state governors in predominantly Christian states promoted

*Jolly Tanko Yusuf welcomes the former president of Tanzania, Julius Nyerere dur-
ing a 1965 visit to Nigeria.*

Islam. Public institutions — the judicial system, newspapers, publishing houses, and radio and television — were forced to operate in ways that promoted Islam and discriminated against Christianity. Christians have been denied access to electronic media in 16 Northern States, while Islam monopolizes 24 hours for its broadcast in the same area. Agents of the devil compound the misery by using the media to heap insults on Christians. Every hour the Muslims broadcast provocative statements about Christianity. It means nothing, they proclaim, that people attend church on Sunday only to dance and listen to songs! Authorities merely wink.

But Sir Bello did not succeed in establishing Islam as the religion of Nigeria. Not at all, even though Muslims would like Nigerians and the world to believe the country has been completely Islamized. But what is more important is that Christians united to stop this pernicious crusade.

Do we expect any fundamental change in Nigeria? If not, then what? Moderate Muslims, not fundamentalists, currently claim to be in the majority in Nigeria. Yet they have hardly come out openly to condemn the fundamentalists who have brought anarchy to Nigeria. While the Izala, a fundamentalist sect, is far from being a majority sect in Nigeria, it exerts much more influence for its size than any other group in the country.

Since its founding (after the 1966 coup d'etat), the Izala sect has dedicated itself to change not only the secular status of Nigeria but also to destroy western and Christian values in the country.

But Nigeria is far more than a nation of Muslims. It is a nation of Christians, Muslims, and citizens who worship God in other ways. Consequently, overwhelming government support for Islam is not only wrong but also dangerous.

Where do we go from here? How long will the Muslim government of Nigeria continue to protect and defend the unjust and show partiality to the wicked?

> "O, God! Do not keep silent,
> be not quiet, O God!
> Be not still.
> Let them know that you,
> whose name is Lord,
> that you alone
> are the most high
> over all the earth."

Diplomacy International

The history of independent Nigeria seems to be measured more by the toppling of regimes than by national elections and completion of statutory terms of presidential office. By the time I had completed 14 years in government, Nigeria had one election, two coups, and one counter coup. Since its birth the nation's development and progress had faltered greatly because of the government's instability and corruption (of which I will speak later).

It was October 1970. Our President, Gen. Yakubu Gowan appointed me High Commissioner of the Federal Republic of Nigeria to Sierra Leone. It was a promotion but it was also a difficult assignment. Comfort and our four younger children (Fatima, Rakiya, Deborah and David) came with me. Our son Ibrahim was born here in 1973.

Sierra Leone's standing among the nations of the world was weak. It believed perhaps that recognition by another country would strengthen its image. Recognizing Biafra, that area of Nigeria engaged in civil war with Nigeria, would provide Sierra Leone, so it reasoned, some esteem with other nations. Gen. Gowan, seeing Sierra Leone's support of Biafra, believed that if the underlying reasons for Nigeria's strife were known to Sierra Leone, it would be neutral.

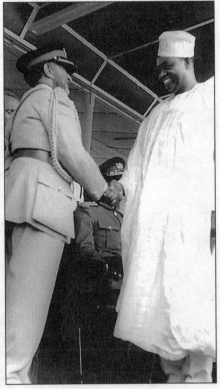

Ambassador Jolly Tanko Yusuf shakes hands with Emperor Haile Selassie during a 1972 visit to Sierra Leone.

Although Nigeria's civil war ended in 1970 while I was in Sierra Leone, I believe I earned the good will of Sierra Leone's government. I had gained the confidence of then-president Honorable Siaka Stevens. Prodded by my belief that we are equal human beings, all of us, and we must value each other, I developed friendship with many people and promoted fellowship between the Sierra Leone people and the many Nigerians living there.

We Nigerians living in Sierra Leone raised funds to construct an additional classroom in a school for the blind and the deaf. We personally helped with the manual labor, often carrying blocks along with the volunteers. My wife Comfort played a leading role. Not only did she care for our children, but also she cooked food and provided refreshing drinks for the workers, and even helped with building the classroom itself. The school stands today.

I visited many old, feeble, or disabled people of the land and, in the name of Nigeria, presented them with gifts and money.

Many Nigerians who lived in Sierra Leone made fortunes from Sierra Leone's diamonds, and the people resented these "foreigners." I persuaded my fellow men that the wealth they acquired from Sierra Leone's assets warranted their contributing to the welfare of its people. Not only had Nigerians made fortunes, but also many of them had married Sierra Leone women, and the people resented this as well.

During a 1973 reception, Yusuf looks on as his wife, Comfort, greets Brig. Gen. Momoh, who later became president of Sierra Leone. Nearby are the Yusufs' three youngest children, from left Fatima, Deborah and Rakiya.

Ambassador Jolly Tanko Yusuf shakes hands with President Siaka Stevens in 1973 in Freetown, Liberia, while Russian Ambassador and Liberia's vice president look on.

Comfort and Jolly Tanko Yusuf sit next to British High Commissioner and his wife at a 1974 State House reception in Sierra Leone.

I held many conferences with Nigerians. Mine was a task of promoting good will. Of course, some jealousies prevailed, but we did understand each other better.

Almost five years later on July 29, 1975, my term here, too, ended suddenly when Gen. Murtala Ramat Muhammed overthrew Gen. Gowan. I left feeling we had made steady progress in traveling the road of neighbor-nations together.

When Gen. Murtala took the reins of Nigeria he immediately fired many civil servants and deployed some as ambassadors to foreign countries, Whether I would be fired, retired, or deployed, I did not know. He ordered me — and several other men — to a meeting in Lagos to learn our fate. It was September 1975. At that meeting I received a letter. I hesitated to open it. I was more than curious. What would the letter say? The letter informed me that Gen. Murtala had deployed me as ambassador — immediately — military fashion, you know — to the People's Republic of China. Nigeria's relationship with China was cordial, and the new assignment excited me. We — Comfort, and our two youngest sons, David and Ibrahim — soon departed Nigeria to begin our new life in China.

China differs greatly from Nigeria. Its history goes back several thousand years. People, food, education, culture, traditions — all were new to me. All challenging. How big was God's world! How more numerous than the sands of the seashore were his creatures. I devoured any information I could find about China, particularly about its cultural revolution and how China had defeated Japan. I traveled extensively.

To govern 1 billion people is a gargantuan task. I was not acquainted with the style of government practiced in China. The government organized people from village to village, town to town, province to province. The country employed a system of central control and collective labor.

Each village had three groups of people: (1) the productive — who had strength enough to work, (2) the elderly, who cared for the children, swept the streets, or did other work that their strength allowed, and (3) Communist Party leaders who served in the hospitals, schools, and other places of leadership and authority.

The Party was above all and everything (this reminded me of Islam's desire in Nigeria). It controlled the producers as well as all other citizens absolutely. The Chinese did not tolerate anyone pointing a dissenting finger at anything Communist or demonstrating any kind of support for democracy and freedom of speech. Could freedom such as we had in Nigeria be successful in China? I think not. The Chinese were not free; the Party ruled absolutely. The Party, members only, met from time to time to elect its leaders and make necessary decisions.

The end of a day's work did not necessarily mean the end of a man or woman's obligations. In the evening the workers attended meetings conducted by Party leaders, who told them what the government wanted them to think and do. Frequently the Party used loud speakers to disseminate information throughout the villages and even in the schoolrooms. The Party controlled what the teachers taught. It articulated the kind of behavior expected from the children and the children learned to obey. Yes, the country was extremely well-organized.

It was also extremely rigid.

As ambassador, I believed I had to look for the good in a country and among its people, and full bellies, I thought, were good. I reflected: Yes, the people lack freedom, but could 1 billion people be as well-nourished as the Chinese under any other system of control and government? Everyone benefited.

Living was crowded and many people squeezed into small rooms. Food was the No. 1 priority. The people were well fed; no one went hungry. I thought about the family of Mao Tse Tung's wife. Her parents had a meager portion of rice only once a day, without salt and without oil. Eventually she became a belly dancer who fell in love with Mao.

I learned to love this people dearly. They are proud of themselves. I loved this land. Their attitude differed from that of people I had met in other countries. Communist laborers organize themselves for production. They obey government orders without questioning. They are docile; they have to be. But, they could be aggressive (although they usually weren't allowed to be). I remember an incident in a shop in Peking (now called Beijing). An American tourist became too bold, and he and a Chinese man began to fight. Fortunately a policeman stepped in and no one was injured.

My life in China was pleasant. Ambassadors occasionally met together for relaxation and enjoyment. I recall an afternoon with Ambassador George Bush from the United States. We were playing golf with a couple of ambassadors from Europe. One said, "George is a winner." Another ambassador then commented that George was a diplomatic winner because he represented the most powerful country in the world! Everybody laughed, and Ambassador Bush chuckled.

Yes, I think of China warmly, even today. On one occasion, after I had retired in Nigeria, I became ill and returned to China for medical treatment. I was given a private room in a Peking hospital, complete with telephone, weekly flowers, and kind care.

In August 1975 Gen. Murtala appointed me Ambassador to the Democratic Peoples Republic of Korea (North Korea), concurrent with my work in China. Less than three months later he added another concurrent assignment, Ambassador to the Socialist Republic of Vietnam. These appointments did not entail too much added work, but they did provide me with freedom to visit these countries. I visited with leaders, presented messages to them from my country, and carried out special assignments.

These three countries gave me a splendid opportunity to observe the socialist system and diplomacy. Much of it I admired, but I detested the denial of the human right to express one's views and feelings. I reported to my government in detail, comparing and contrasting the governments and societies of these three countries with Nigeria. I made many positive suggestions to my government. My report seemed constructive to President Gen. Olusegun Obasanjo — Gen. Murtala's successor — and he sent a six-man delegation to see me in Peking.

Unfortunately I was in New Delhi, attending a meeting of the Nigerian ambassadors who were then serving in Asia. There I received word of the delegation in Peking; I would have to return to Peking. With no available direct flight from New Delhi to Peking, I almost circled the globe on my return. I flew to Tokyo, Alaska, Tehran, and finally Peking. I met with the President's six-man delegation led by Nigeria's Minister of Agriculture. The senior delegate complimented me on my excellent report and said the President had found it comprehensive and its suggestions constructive. The suggestions, he said, should be followed promptly.

They never were.

Late in 1978 I finally returned to Nigeria. I looked forward to retiring and living quietly.

But God had other plans.

17

Politics Again

If I had any idea about quietly settling down it soon vanished.

I had hardly readjusted to life in Nigeria when some of my close friends and political colleagues asked me to join the National Party of Nigeria (NPN), formed in 1978. The NPN, predominantly influenced by Muslims, was similar to NPC, but it was a political party. What could I do in the NPN, I wondered. I had already observed that the Muslims had ingratiated themselves into federal agencies, economics, the legal system, and other institutions of authority in Nigeria. I was alarmed. Could my participation — perhaps — help move the political influence towards freedom for all? I joined. I was elected chairman of Gongola State, of which Takum was a part. I hoped that the NPN would be a party that would accommodate all tribes and religions.

I was one of the six members of a task force requested to introduce President Shahu Shagari and his plans to the people. I assured the people the President would uphold equal rights for all religions, and we all should support him. I assured the people that President Shagari would not change his ideas and actions.

But he did.

I resigned early in 1983.

In 1980 President Shagari, who was the first civilian to be elected after 12 years of military rule, appointed me Special Assistant to the President to serve in Kaduna State. A special assistant was responsible for the oversight of federal agencies and institutions in a state. He also handled federal affairs and reported political and economic conditions of his state to the President. I accepted reluctantly; I sensed the relationships between the Kaduna government and me would not be smooth, because the governor of the state was of the opposing party.

Indeed, the two years I spent in Kaduna were difficult and unpleasant. The President and I had agreed that we would work together and there would be no religious discrimination. I soon discovered that President Shagari did not take my suggestions or advice seriously. Why then, I wondered, had he appointed me? I watched corruption in Kaduna and Nigeria mount. I saw rampant nepotism and blatant discrimination. I observed that Sharia (Islamic law that regulated all of human life) was fast becoming the law of the land.

I learned too that the President had appointed a Special Assistant for Religious Affairs in Nigeria without informing me. I happened to see a letter routed to Alhaji Abubakar Gumi, the leader of the Izala sect. He was the man who "did not want to hear the word Christian in Nigeria"! I suspected that his main duty would be to work towards Islamization of our country. The fact that the President did not also appoint anyone to be a Special Assistant for the Christian religion substantiated my suspicions. When I realized what was going on without my knowledge, I pleaded with the President to replace me. He refused; he knew the political fallout would embarrass him.

I stayed on.

The situation did not improve. With a government that readily promoted Islam at the expense of Christianity and encouraged corruption, my agitation grew. In 1983 when he refused my advice to remove three corrupt ministers regarded by the public as notorious, I resigned again. I wrote my letter of resignation in a way that left no room for my retraction. The vice president advised President Shagari to reject my resignation because people might think it would indicate that something was wrong in government. The President said, "I know Jolly. When he says no, he means no."

Before I resigned I did have the opportunity to tell the President, in the presence of two friends and special assistants to the president, that the army would come back again if corruption were not curtailed. President Shagari's close friends surrounded him and formed a very powerful caucus that controlled his politics. They regarded as crime any opposing political opinion or any advice against corruption and vices in government.

When news of my resignation reached the public, what was expected happened. People were really concerned, and this disgust exploded in many areas. Many people insinuated that I should not blame the President for what was happening in Nigeria. But they were blind; they did not see the handwriting on the wall. They did not see that he was leading Nigeria to disaster.

In spite of the political fallout, I did not regret my resignation. I detest military coups. If a president is removed from office, he should be replaced by the people via a national election. But it was a coup, in December of 1983, that vindicated my resignation.

As a result of this coup, Gen. Mohammed Buhari now became Nigeria's president. It was expected. He started out positively and seemed to understand what Nigeria needed. With his "War Against Indiscipline," he tried diligently to introduce discipline among the people, urging them to work hard on the job without pushing one another. However, the people felt that the President was too stern and that he allowed his colleagues too much power to oppress people. People did not tolerate this. Another coup! This one in 1985. President Buhari's military colleagues overthrew him.

Because my opposition to Muslim domination was both visible and vocal, it became obvious that my Christian principles and background formed the basis of my outspoken convictions. This no doubt contributed to the general Muslim impression that Jolly Tanko Yusuf of the Middle Belt was indeed "a difficult man" — as newspapers, magazines, and radio frequently said. During the late '80s it was also convenient for many to think that I had created Nigeria's problems. On one occasion, while I was hospitalized in London, a Nigerian newspaper, "The Reporter," wrote that I was among those who urged the killing of Muslims. (How little they knew me!) They then linked the opposition to CAN.

From this date on I was seen as a controversial person.

Which I accepted.

As representative of Nigeria, Ambassador Jolly Tanko Yusuf and his wife, Comfort, welcome Pope John II during a 1981 visit.

18

The Christian Association of Nigeria

Amid the consternation that swirled around me in the early days of my anticipated "quiet retirement," my thoughts turned to the Christian Association of Nigeria (CAN).

It was not difficult to see that the purpose and benefits of CAN provided a way for Christians of all of Nigeria to band together. It had been formed while I was in China, but it seemed to me a bit lethargic. It was not moving, politically speaking, and it was high time for Christians to become a political force.

Although there were many reasons for the formation of CAN, one particular incident made Christian leaders realize vividly the threat of Islam and that the effect of Christian denominations on Nigerian government and politics was minimal. It happened at a government-sponsored meeting in Lagos. Nigeria's vice president, according to Rev. Habila chaired the meeting. The vice president called on a Muslim to say prayers before and after this meeting. Although both Christians and Muslims were attending the meeting, the Christian leaders were overlooked.

One Christian stood up and asked, "Can't you ask a Christian to say a prayer?"

The vice president said, "There are so many denominations represented here, how can I ask any Christian to say a prayer?"

The Rev. Bagaya of the Sudan Interior Missions was the first chairman of the Northern Christian Association.

At the official inauguration of the Northern Christian Association in 1964, the
Rev. Habila Aleyediono, deputy chairman, offers a prayer.

One of the bishops raised his hand and said, "Any one from any of the
denominations represented here can say a prayer for all."

Then the vice president did give a Christian leader permission to ask a
bishop to lead in prayer, which he did.

After the meeting, several Christians walked out together. One suggested that they go to the Catholic Center in Lagos to talk: "See what has happened? Why don't we have unity as the Muslims have? Why don't we have
a united forum? Aren't we united?" Christians are united in Christ, of
course, but too often we do not act on it.

Rev. Habila explained to the other Christians then that a Christian organization, the Northern Christian Association (NCA), already existed in the
north. Further, he said, it included people from all Christian denominations;
it sought to unite Christians politically, regardless of denominational or tribal differences. The idea of NCA was very good. Its purpose corresponded
with Christ's admonition that we Christians unite and live in unity with him.

NCA, he told them, had even received the support of mission organizations. In a letter (April 17, 1964) to members of the Council of Evangelical
Churches of Northern Nigeria, its secretary, Rev. Smith had written,

"… at its formation there were Christians present of every denomination, not a few of them holding high positions in our churches … this Association has a two-fold aim; to safeguard the interests of the Christians and
to promote the spread of the gospel …. They do not wish Missions or expatriates which are of foreign origin to be embarrassed by what is happening

Jolly Tanko Yusuf as president of the Northern Christian Association in 1964. Later, he was Coordinator and National Vice President of CAN 1980–1989.

John A.T. Orume, assistant general secretary of the Northern Christian Association.

to their own Nigerian brethren. They prefer to take care of these matters themselves.... I wish to urge that we who are from other lands respect this bold effort of our brethren ... and by continual prayer ... encourage them to work out their own salvation."

At that time Mallam E. B. Mamiso, one of the provincial commissioners (Resident Minister) of Sardauna and Benue Provinces, and I informed Sir Bello by a private and personal letter (April 10, 1964) of the formation of the Northern Christian Association:

"We as beloved sons of yours in whom you have confidence, feel duty bound to make our contribution to safeguard the interest of our beloved mother North which you are destined to lead. And it is with this objective of 'One North, one people, irrespective of tribe, religion or rank' that we decided to get all Northern Christians indirectly having their own separate Christian Association; in order to stop some Southern opportunists from wedging our age-old solidarity in Northern Nigeria."

That a Christian organization existed cheered the concerned Christian leaders attending the meeting, and now they finally woke up. Some years later (in 1978 or 1979) NCA formally changed its name to the Christian Association of Nigeria (CAN). Now Christians from not only the north but also from the east and west could and did begin to work together.

Of course, this expansion didn't make the Muslims happy. They wanted Nigeria to be a theocratic state, Islamic style. Since the era of Sir Bello, the Sardauna of Sokoto, Muslims had left no stone unturned in their attempt to establish an Islamic theocracy. Sir Bello had claimed thousands of converts. The late Mallam Makaman Bidda said on the floor of the Northern House of Assembly:

"Sardauna is a leader who believes in God, and therefore all his enemies wherever they may be are enemies of God and God will punish them one by one."

He made this statement after the inauguration of the NCA in 1964. The NCA had, from its beginning, a formidable task.

However, since the CAN convention in Kaduna in 1987, which was attended by many members of the House of Representatives, including the vice president, and by the Senate president, I felt greatly encouraged. Even optimistic.

CAN had come alive again. It started to move, but deciding what

Representatives of many denominations meet in Enugu at the first meeting of the Christian Association of Nigeria.

action to take — and doing it — wasn't easy. People in the south did not understand the need for political cooperation and had to be persuaded that unity was more important than tribalism. They didn't realize that a united voice was stronger than a chorus of dissident voices from every part of the country.

At this time, I was a rank-and-file member of CAN. Unity among Christians of every tribe became my consuming mindset. Now retired, I had free time to use, and I gave much — no, most — of it to CAN. Not being violent, I wanted to go ahead peacefully and constitutionally. I traveled. Taught. Preached. Discussed. Involved myself in peaceful demonstration. I have done this since 1984 and still continue today. I traveled throughout all of Nigeria, mostly driving in my faithful Peugeot.

Unity! Unity! Unity! Any way I could think of. I passionately wanted Nigeria to be truly independent and democratic. It occupied my thoughts, my prayer, my life. I tried to enlighten people, both Christians and non-Christians. To Christians I preached unity in Christ above tribalism and denominational squabbles, explaining that the only real unity humankind will ever know is unity in Christ Jesus. To non-Christian men and women of good will I emphasized the need for a secular government (and surely not an Islamic government, with all that it would mean) in a pluralistic country such as ours. Without it our beloved country will not, cannot survive.

When in 1986 the Nigerian government joined the Organization of Islamic Conference (OIC) without the consent of the people, I was incensed. I became even more vocal. I saw that with increasing force Islam was impinging on the freedom of religion in democratic Nigeria, and I believed we Christians had to protect our faith from Islam. In a democracy there must be freedom of religion, not merely for Islam but also for Christians.

Because Muslim fundamentalists believed they alone were holy and totally loyal to the teachings of the Qu'ran, non-fundamentalist and non-extremist Muslims may well appreciate CAN for forcing fundamentalists to see that religion is indeed a personal affair and cannot be legislated. Moderate Muslims, like Christians, could see that in multi-tribal, multi-religious Nigeria the law has to acknowledge that religion is personal. Only as one's personal beliefs direct his or her conduct for the good of all the people, with discrimination towards none, can they be used to provide rationale and direction for the various branches of government. (Of course, political and selfish interests also affect freedom of religion, and discrimination based on politics can never be completely ruled out.)

Because of my activities for CAN and for Nigeria, I was elected vice president of CAN in 1988. This election broke a record; it was the first time that CAN chose a layman to be No. 2 in the organization. Nevertheless, I now accepted the challenge and spent all my time recruiting members and persuading them of the seriousness of Nigeria's politics.

Politics are never smooth, clean, unruffled. Sometimes intrigue, deceit, and corruption gnaw at the very core of an organization. In 1982 something happened that made me unhappy. The federal government planned to build a mosque in Abuja. Many Muslim countries in the Middle East had already donated large sums of money towards the building, but additional money would be needed from the government to complete the construction. Through various sources I had learned of these ongoings, and I urged certain people who had important contact with the government to suggest, rather forcibly, that the government should treat Christians in equal fashion. Then the government let it be known that a cathedral would also be built in Abuja, with N10 million to be contributed by the government to Christians (through CAN). Church leaders did not like subterfuge one bit and rather than calling the proposed building a cathedral, they designated it an Ecumenical Center. I was appointed chairman of the building committee.

Then something happened!

At first, though, it was not apparent. Because we could not build immediately, the N10 million was deposited in the bank, but because of inflation its value had decreased greatly. CAN's executive committee explained this decrease in value to Gen. Babangida, who was now President. We told him we did not have nearly enough money to build the center.

The government then gave another N30 million to CAN's executive secretary, who was the trustee. I was not informed of this additional gift. He placed the money in a bank so that the account would draw interest.

Two Christian bank employees saw that something unusual was happening to CAN's money. They reported their observations to a Christian businessman: Some Muslim employees had been discussing the discrepancies in the CAN account. And further, Jolly Tanko Yusuf's name was connected to the skimming. This had been going on for four months.

The businessman came to my home and charged that Christian leaders were taking CAN's money. I asked him for copies of the deposit transactions, which I received a month later. The letters of deposit showed that an additional N30 million had indeed been deposited. The letter of deposit indicated that the money would draw 24 percent interest, instead of 27 percent as the bank had previously offered.

What had happened to the 3 percent?

That difference was lining someone's pocket. Whose? I didn't know. More than a quarter million naira in interest had been skimmed from our account. And we had proof. With it I went to Lagos to visit CAN's national president. At first he said he couldn't believe it, but then I asked him to read four letters of bank transactions, which he did. He said he didn't know of the interest reduction. I didn't believe him; it simply could not have been done without the organization's leaders knowing it. And I knew I hadn't known about it.

I returned to Kaduna and wrote him a letter. I recommended that the money be returned to the family of Jesus and that all the accounts now on deposit in this bank be transferred to a bank paying higher interest. My letter, of course, was a challenge. But surely, if we Christians criticized our corrupt leaders, then Christian leaders should not themselves be corrupt.

It was a crisis.

The rumor of cheating was spreading. Eventually the matter reached CAN'S executive committee. At a meeting called for this purpose, CAN's secretary general was allowed to speak, but he disregarded the agenda and the order of business. He specifically attacked my integrity and said he didn't like me, and the Anglican bishop of Abuja was backing me; therefore he was going to resign. The president did not allow me to reply.

I knew something devious was brewing. The president was irritated when I commented that his denying me the right to speak was unusual. After finishing the agenda, however, he finally allowed me to speak. I addressed the general secretary, asking, "What was my crime?" He couldn't name it.

I was dismayed. I believed accountability should be the watchword of all Christian leaders. I did learn later the stolen money had already been returned to CAN's president, who still claimed he knew nothing about the skimming.

I felt I could no longer continue as an officer of CAN. Originally CAN's constitution had required "priests of high standing" as officers. The constitution was changed during the OIC controversy (the President's making Nigeria a member of the Organization of Islamic Conference without the consent of the citizenry). The change, I recall, had been made so that I could become CAN's national vice president. I personally had been deeply involved in the OIC controversy and leadership in CAN would give my role legitimacy.

And now I resigned.

I recommended that they not continue with a layman vice president. Suppose something happened to the president, I suggested, the vice president would become the chief officer. A new vice president was elected at CAN's next meeting. I did not attend but I did send my recommendation. (I did not know then that CAN was planning to return the constitution to its original qualifications for officers.)

I decided to continue as CAN's coordinator of 16 northern states and Abuja. Before the reversion of its constitution in 1989 Catholics and the Council of Churches in Nigeria controlled CAN. The new churches (TEKAN and EKWA) were not recognized, nor were the Youth organization and the Women's section. I fought to change the constitution to recognize the others, and this did happen a bit later. We have one Bible and one Jesus and it is important that CAN recognize this not only in word but in action.

Even though I no longer was an officer of CAN, my loyalty to it and its purpose did not decrease. I continued my efforts to strengthen the unity among Christians particularly emphasizing membership in CAN. I directed most of my effort to the southern part of the country and partly in the east. Some areas knew nothing about CAN. I toured towns and villages, worshipped in their churches, and talked with the people by means of seminars and symposiums in universities, churches, and more.

Wherever I could find a group of people, particularly women and youth, I spoke. Committed Christian women are invaluable. Their yes means yes and their no means no. When they say they will do something they do it! The Christian youth of today are our leaders and our hope for tomorrow. I felt deeply that without winning both the women and the youth, CAN would not survive.

The government saw me as the Christian nuisance who realized that the country was indeed becoming more and more Islamic. And further, I was traveling the country and

Ambassador Jolly Tanko Yusuf addresses the Christian Association of Nigeria in 1980.

enlightening the people about what was happening. I fought against Nigeria becoming part of the OIC. I fought against the introduction of Sharia as the law of the land. I was angry.

I became a target of the government.

Discrimination against Christians was rampant. It never stopped. They were being deprived of their full rights and were being overlooked for appointments and civil service. It disturbed me deeply that our country was missing the services of hundreds of talented, educated, and dedicated young citizens. It pleased me that the younger folks were waking up to the tragedy and joining our struggle. People joined CAN in many, many sections of the country where CAN branches had not yet been established. I continued my efforts until 1991.

And then I was arrested.

It was a rainy night in Kaduna. I was taking my daily walk. On my return home I learned that the secretary of Youth CAN of Kaduna had been arrested. I went to headquarters to find out why — and I too was arrested! Almost immediately the people knew something was happening. The police tried to whisk me away without notice, but as we neared the gate to Lagos (where I was to be detained), I noticed a crowd of people milling around. As the car pulled nearer to the crowd, many women dropped onto the ground ahead of the car.

I shouted to the driver, "Stop! If you kill them God will kill you." I jerked his hand back.

No one was hurt, thank God. The driver went to another gate safely. I was soon taken to Lagos.

For two months the authorities held me for being so actively involved in CAN. Actually the struggle had already started three decades earlier. Hadn't I — and many others, of course — been actively trying to make all of Nigeria aware of the extent to which the Muslims were attempting to control Nigeria? I became a visible target.

Therefore when Maj. Gideon Okar, a young Tiv, attempted (unsuccessfully) a coup against Gen. Babangida, he and his cohorts thought I was the brain behind it. The first statement of the major had been that some Muslim-dominated parts of the country should cut ties completely with the Muslim north. Because Muslims have the illusion that I don't like them, they alleged that I had written that speech for Maj. Okar, that I too favored excising part of the country. Perpetrators of the failed coup, I knew, had been put to death. I wondered what would happen to me.

Based on that charge I, along with several other Christians, was arrested at midnight and taken to Lagos. The government wanted to frighten me into silence. CAN was too successful for them, especially now that it had become national and its influence had expanded. I told them I would never stop; I would rather die than be silent.

Military intelligence held us in Apapa for two nights and then moved us to Security Service (SS) headquarters in Ikoyi, Lagos, for further questioning. At first our quarters were not crowded. But before our time was spent, 23 of us were sleeping in one room, on the floor on narrow mattresses. Although crowded, the room was clean. It had no facilities besides water. The officers ignored my constitutional rights, but that didn't bother my Islamic captors. They knew exactly what they were doing and why. They wanted my silence. I knew they couldn't keep up this inquisition about the attempted coup and my alleged part in it. When time for my release came, the military dictator, Gen. Ibrahim Babangida sent the former head of state, Gen. Gowan, to talk with me. After that the SS boss took me to the residence of the chief of the army, Gen. Sani Abacha, where I met with him, Major Generals Dogon Yaro, Kure, and Haledu, and SS Chief Alhaji Samaila.

I asked, "Why are you holding me? What have I done?" "We have found nothing," they replied. "Gen. Babangida has told us to apologize to you. You are free."

"Why haven't you arrested Alhaji Gumi?" I asked. "Doesn't he want to divide the country?" Gumi was such a strong and active Muslim agitator. He had said quite openly that if Christians were to rule, the country should be divided because he could not accept Christians as leaders! He had profaned the name of my Jesus, which I could not tolerate. Yet he remained free. I concluded that behind the scenes Gumi was the "Ayatollah of Nigeria."

When they said I was released, I insisted they also release the other Christians who were being held in various places because of me and because of their faith. Without their release, I would remain in jail.

"They are your disciples," the interrogator said.

I replied vehemently, "No indeed. They are not my disciples. I am a human being, an ordinary person. They and I are disciples of Jesus Christ."

My captors got the message and spoke to the President the same day. In about one week, all of us in Lagos, Kaduna, and other states were released.

Our detention did not go unnoticed. The demonstrations were reported widely in the media, and the work of CAN and the Christians received great publicity. This the Muslims had not intended!

CAN continued to be my channel of choice.

Alhaji Abubakar Gumi

With no authority except that which he had assumed for himself, Alhaji Abubakar Gumi, leader of Izala, has directed young Nigeria's efforts toward an Islam-dominated oligarchy more than any other person except perhaps Sir Ahmadu Bello and Gen. Ibrahim Badamasi Babangida. On one occasion he said that if Nigeria became a two-party nation it "will not be South against North any longer but Islam against Christianity." (Free Nation, Dec. 1988, p. 12).

The Jama'atu Izalatu Bidi'a Wa Igmatus Sunna (or Izala), was founded by Gumi shortly after the 1966 coup. It dedicated itself to change Nigeria's secular status and to destroy western and Christian values in the country in order to become a strictly Muslim country. Gumi believed he could and would easily be accepted as leader of the North and so fill the vacuum left by Sir Bello's death. He has tried everything, including control of government machinery such as the Federal Radio Corp. in Kaduna (FRC) and television, to establish a new political system based upon the fundamental precepts of Islam.

Even after the reconciliation of differences between Izala and other renowned Muslim scholars of pure minds, Gumi refused to accept any efforts of emirs, chiefs, civilian and military administrations to make peace. Genuine scholars object to Gumi's interpretation of the Qu'ran and insist that Gumi's teaching is contrary to the precepts of Islam. Gradually Gumi won the minds of the "unintelligent" educated Muslim elite, including military officers, university professors, and others.

Izala has continually preached the gospel of violence. Disturbances in many cities in the northern states from 1972 to date have resulted in the loss of many lives and much property. One wonders, though, why the authorities, especially law enforcement agents, have remained silent over Izala's criminal activities. It is common knowledge that the Nigerian police and other authorities have the full facts concerning Izala's criminal activities.

Gumi made his most dangerous public statement in February 1976 (when Gen. Murtala Muhammed was assassinated) after prayer at Sultan Bello Mosque in Kaduna. He lamented that Nigerian Muslims have now lost a "Muslim leader" and that the world will say that any country having at least 12,000 Muslims but not a Muslim leader is a "non-Muslim country."

That statement indicated Gumi's intent to incite violence between Muslims and Christians, since Gen. Obasinjo, the man who succeeded Murtala, was a Christian. During his three years in office, he demonstrated the Christian "liberalism" of allowing all faiths and peoples to live together equally and peaceably. In 1978 Nigeria had an election, and Gen. Obasinjo peaceably handed the government to the new President. He made history!

Gumi's inflammatory speech, however, did not create the reaction that was expected. Still, the belief is gaining ground among some fanatics (including the unintelligent educated elite) that the founder of Izala was an Allah-sent Messiah whose duty it was to correct other Muslims and to Islamize Nigeria.

In his sermons, this self-styled Ayatollah encouraged his disciples to join the Nigerian army, police forces, and other armed services, not particularly to serve the nation but to learn war tactics with a view to taking over the country one day. According to recorded evidence, on Aug. 27, 1982, he openly incited the public against both the government and the people of Nigeria who do not believe that religion should not be used for political purposes.

Yusuf greets Archbishop Peter Jatau as Sheikh Abubakar Gumi and Alhaji Isa Kaita look on, at a 1991 joint meeting of Christian and Muslim leaders in Government House, Kawo.

He has employed other methods too. For example, an Islamic equiva-lent of the Red Cross has been established in some parts of Nigeria. It plans to build separate hospitals for Muslim communities alongside Mus-lim schools that already exist.

Izala's objectives violated Section 10 (30) of the Nigerian Constitution. Izala aimed to make Islam the country's state religion and the Qu'ran its constitution. Izala's fanatic strategies included a show of power and vio-lence not only against Christians, but against other Muslims who refused to join them. Izala's propaganda for the need of Jihad (religious war against non-believers) seriously threatened law and order in our country.

The claim that government had a lukewarm attitude towards the increasing religious intolerance is not far-fetched because now Izala has been accepted by many Muslim scholars, some of whom hold key posi-tions in government and the armed forces. Has this made Gumi a sacred cow? Not only Christians fear the reckless activities of Izala. Muslims of other sects also fear. There are more than 10 other Islamic sects besides the real majority Darika sect and the fundamentalist group led by Gumi. The terror of the 1982 Kano Maitatisine (the leader) riots among the Mus-lims themselves, was fresh in the minds of the people of Nigeria.

Gumi is never quiet. At the Aniagolu Tribunal, set up to investigate the Kano riots, Gumi defended Izala during the Tribunal's sitting. He later retracted his comments on Radio Kaduna. He poked his nose into the Ahmadu Bello University religious disturbances in 1981, using his organi-zation to incite students by inscribing indelible provocative words (such as ISLAM ONLY) on public buildings. Such abuse of power is un-Christian and must be corrected within the concepts of Christianity. Since 1978 and with the emergence of Izala, Nigeria has experienced many religious crises and riots, including the assault and flagrant attacks on the Christian faith, which reached their climax in March 1987. An ominous violence erupted on the day that the Nigerian "King Faisal Laureate," Sheik Abubakar Gumi returned from Saudi Arabia. His return tended to confirm the fear of Christians that foreign powers, especially the OIC member-states and their Nigerian collaborators wanted to Islamize Nigeria at all cost. The silence of government did not help alleviate this fear.

Although not directly a tool of Jihad, the 1987 Muslim-provoked Kano riots became a major tragedy. Christian communities were stunned as their chapels, churches, institutions, centers and private properties went up in flames, and brothers and sisters were set ablaze on church premises and streets. One hundred fifty-four churches and houses, in addition to cars, motorcycles and other valuables, were set on fire. In four days (March 9–13, 1987), 19 persons were known to have been killed, and N75 million worth of property was destroyed. Broken-hearted Christians did nothing, but they asked God for wisdom to avoid vengeance, because vengeance belongs to God.

It seems that both the law and the government were unwilling to defend the Christian community during the brutal assault on churches and the property of Christians in Kaduna, Kafanchan, Zaria, Kankia, and other places during the 1987 March riots. This was taken by Christians and others to clearly indicate that the OIC has a grand design to destabilize the country and take it over.

Izala's extreme sense of religious superiority continues to create problems, not only in Nigeria but in other Islamic countries as well. Some groups of Iranian fundamentalists are known to have caused the riot that claimed more than 300 lives during the 1987 pilgrimage to Mecca. Other known Islamic groups, whose philosophy seems to be hooliganism, believe such actions contradict true Islamic faith. Moderate Muslims claim they, not the fundamentalists, are the majority. To the dismay of many, however, these moderate Muslims have not publicly condemned the fundamentalists who nearly brought anarchy to Nigeria.

Other religious extremists similar to Gumi teach, preach and practice doctrines taught by Iran's Ayatollah. Islamic fanaticism ridicules the Christian faith in Nigeria.

However, Christians are not innocent. Some Christians preach and practice doctrines that are the antithesis of Christian faith. They call to question the faithfulness of Christians who do not subscribe to the teachings and interpretations of the Bible as these extremists teach it. Some Christians have become so complacent they do not recognize distorted interpretation of God's Word.

We Christians need strong spiritual unity. Personal interests may not blind Christians to situations that call for uncompromising action against injustice, corruption, nepotism, and violence. Christians must oppose Gumi. They have no choice.

The flagrant abuse of power by Gumi and his followers does not permit neutrality in government. In addition it is extremely anti-Christian. The fundamental difference between the behavior of Muslims and Christians is the difference between force and love. God still assures Christians that he loves the world (John 3:16), and that he still controls this world. Zechariah said (4:6), "Not by power, nor by might, but by my Spirit, says the Lord." Or, as John has challenged Christians, "There is no fear in love, but perfect love casts out fear" (I John 18).

Ibrahim Badamasi Babangida

That infamous day — August 27, 1985 — dawned sunny in Nigeria's young life. Most of our days are like that. But the day soon lost its luster.

Another military coup! On this day Gen. Ibrahim Badamasi Babangida overthrew Gen. Buhari's government. Gen. Buhari's government was none too popular, true. Gen. Babangida's was worse. The oppressed Nigerian citizenry, so tired of Gen. Buhari's "War Against Indiscipline," listened to Gen. Babangida at first, even though it might have brought some sanity and healthy change in Nigeria.

But did Gen. Babangida bring light and hope? No. Eight years after he commandeered the presidency, the darkness of mismanagement and evil still crippled Nigeria. We yearned for the morning of honesty and equality in government.

Not until June 12, 1993, would Nigeria have another election by the people. Mallam Moshood K.O. Abiola won that election with an overwhelming majority. Hardly were the votes counted when Gen. Babangida nullified the election, claiming "the election was rigged." Again the people were denied representation.

We, the people, had looked forward with hope to an election by the people. We Christians had prayed for a moderate President. For eight years now Gen. Babangida had ruled Nigeria with evil fervor. Along with nullifying the election, Gen. Babangida appointed an interim government, so his henchmen still remain in power.

At first when Gen. Babangida engineered the coup that catapulted him into the office of President, citizens anticipated healthy change. Changes there were, but healthy they were not. In some ways the early popularity of Gen. Babangida's military junta reminded me of Adolph Hitler's early popularity in Germany. At first Hitler seemed to understand his country; he sympathized with poor and victimized people. So did Gen. Babangida, or so we were led to believe. Hitler portrayed himself as "a man of the people." So did Gen. Babangida. The people saw Hitler as the leader who personally could lift Germany from its plight. But everyone who knows history knows the rest of that terrible era.

The hope that Gen. Babangida brought — in spite of the way he took office — was soon dashed. His publicized "vision" gained no respect. His promises were empty. He assumed authority by force.

His popularity quickly vanished in his raw abuse of his office. He used every trick and pretense to grab more and more power. He preached peace and practiced conflict. He recklessly abused the authority of his high office.

He relied heavily on the advice of the powerful Council of Ulama (a Muslim think tank) and Gumi who, of course, represented only Muslim extremists. Based on its interpretation of the Qu'ran, Ulama revised standing rules and regulations and drafted new federal policies. Gen. Babangida declared Ulama's recommendations to be policy. The objectives of Ulama, so quietly fashioned and cleverly implemented, are now firmly embedded in government regulations and directions.

Gen. Babangida arbitrarily interfered with the democratic process whenever possible. I recall a 1987 meeting of the Constituent Assembly in Abuja called especially to revise the Nigerian Constitution. The delegates were debating whether the Sharia did or did not relate to the Constitution. They were nearing a resolution of this important and very troublesome problem.

Suddenly and without warning, Gen. Babangida shocked the Assembly! His second-in-command appeared at the door and rudely stopped the debate, wresting the entire subject from the competent hands of the peoples' representatives.

Acting as though the government had not authorized the Assembly, he said, "Your work is finished. The matter has been placed in the hands of 19 newly selected members of the Armed Forces Ruling Council (AFRC)." It was Nigerian's highest governmental body; it decides the future of 90 million Nigerians. These 19 men later inserted into the Constitution the phrases and clauses they desired.

Where was Gen. Babangida during this travesty? In West Africa, on a visit. When he returned he announced that the inclusion of specific Sharia provisions in the 1979 Constitution was adequate.

Did Christians recognize this political deceit? Of course. Gen. Babangida had pressured these men to retain the Sharia in the constitution to appease his Muslim brothers. The subsequent Constitutional Revision Commission recommendations on Sharia and the Customary (civil) Courts of Appeal confirmed his intent.

Its work having been so abruptly halted, the chairman of the original Constituent Assembly then presented an unfinished draft of the revised Constitution to Gen. Babangida. The draft, however, retained the old wording of Sharia. "It would have been untidy to leave blank spaces in the draft-constitution when we submitted it to the government," the chairman explained.

To avoid embarrassment to unwilling members of the Constituent Assembly, only the chairman and the secretary had signed the draft Constitution. With the old Sharia provisions retained, Christians and other sensible members (who together formed the majority) would not have signed the document anyway. In fact, all the maneuvers and manipulations were designed to prevent Christians from using their majority to embarrass Gen. Babangida's government.

The government itself had tried to force the Assembly to leave blank spaces in the draft. When Gen. Babangida found the spaces in the Constitution filled with obsolete provisions, he requested a new chairman to insert the correct Sharia version in proper places.

How transparent it is that our government is determined to elevate Islam from among the ranks of many active religions in Nigeria to the position of the state religion. A few inept sycophants, who believe in the supremacy of a particular tribe or religion, are trying to destroy the people's freedom to follow their own religions.

One man's lust for power has denied human rights to the majority of Nigeria's millions. Such mockery of the people cannot long withstand the silent rebellion that smolders just beneath the surface of the nation's people.

In June 1987 Gen. Babangida established an Advisory Council on Religious Affairs (ACRA). This Council, he explained, would promote moral values in Nigerian society and encourage cordial relations among Nigeria's various religious groups. He appointed me as a member. I accepted.

Later I discovered that the purpose of the men in power was to promote the Islamic religion and Sharia through whatever means possible. This council provided one way! I saw that the Advisory Council would be cosmetic only, and I could not in good conscience be part of it.

I resigned after the first meeting that followed the Council's inauguration. Later the Council itself collapsed.

Islam continues to make inroads even though Jihad is no longer waged by sword. It doesn't have to. Those agents of the devil compound people's misery by using electronic and print media to heap insults on Christians.

Ulama, of course, brashly blames Christians not only for inciting disturbances but also for persecuting Muslims! The Nigerian Army, Ulama says, does not intervene to resolve crises but to defend Christians. Ridiculous! Young Christians aren't that numerous in Nigeria's army; they find it difficult even to be accepted! How unfair and unfortunate! Gen. Babangida and state governors are concerned only with their own positions. Not one, not one visited any of the properties and churches burned during the

1987 Kano riots. Not one visited any of the families of persons killed by Muslim rioters.

The Christian asks: Is it wise and safe that the institution that bears responsibility of defending all its citizens to recruit only Muslims? Does Ulama not realize that its brazenly hostile attitude towards Christians and Christian soldiers may have long-term evil consequences for the very survival of Nigeria?

Gen. Babangida's government has claimed to be democratic, yet it continually ignores democratic principles. In no way does our government represent all the people. Muslims, who occupy most of the important positions in the government, follow a "help-your-own-people" policy. Gen. Babangida closes his eyes and shuts his ears to the cries of hurting people.

At no time has a government official or employee been investigated for corruption. Nor has our government ever clarified a suspicious or disturbing situation to remove the people's mistrust. Even some of the country's inimitable social critics (like Tai Solarin, for example, who wrote on the missing N2.8 billion during Shagari's rule) could not reverse the ungodly rot and corruption of government at all levels.

Only Christians, with God's help, and concerned citizens can.

The Challenge

When Gen. Babangida threw out President-elect Abiola on the day after the election in June 1993, he placed another roadblock in our journey toward the promised land of the Third Republic. Will we crouch behind it or destroy it? May we huddle, speechless, behind the roadblock of corruption and military abuse while Nigeria plunges onward to its own destruction? The battle with corrupt government and Islamic control is fierce. Yet we must continue to "give to Caesar what is Caesar's and to God what is God's." (Mt. 22:21)

Jesus Christ demands that Christians be responsible citizens, neither antagonistic toward government nor allowing its rot. We seek not to destroy Islam but rather to elect a government that will allow all Nigerians (Christians, Muslims, and traditionalists) freedom to follow the religion of their conscience without fear of discrimination or violence.

Huddled passively behind a roadblock will not bring change.

The time for change is NOW. Are we Christians and other people of good will ready? What then shall we do?

Two things, basically. First, we must unite in Jesus Christ as he himself has commanded in John 17, that we may be one with him and the father. Second, united together, with strength born of conviction, we must become active in Nigerian government and politics.

The real hope of any nation is people living together in harmony, particularly Christian harmony. My thoughts often turn to Adam and Eve. Created perfect, to complement one another, they nevertheless disobeyed God. Broken was their beautiful unity! God saw the awfulness of their disobedience and mercifully provided a way for men and women to regain it. He sent Jesus Christ to make unity possible again. Jesus prayed, "... that they may be one as we are one; I in them and you in me. May they be brought to complete unity ..." (John 17:22-23)

Unity is hard work. Jesus suffered all his life for it. Betrayed for money. Spat upon. Whipped. Scorned. Mocked. Crucified! Why? He was honest, and dared to stand against the immoralities of his time; he condemned the hypocrisies of both Gentiles and Jews. He lived his role: to bring salvation for humankind. To restore unity!

The Christian church, ideally, represents the epitome of unity. Church is the Body of Jesus Christ. The diversity among Nigeria's 300-plus tribes and languages, on the other hand, make harmony and unity difficult. Churches, unfortunately, too easily dismiss harmony as an impossible, perhaps even undesirable, dream. Unless the church encourages tolerance, love, and unity above denomination or tribal loyalty, who will?

Too often churches, even within a single denomination, misunderstand one another. They ought not criticize each other but rather capitalize on the strengths of each other. They ought not to be indifferent to one another but rather be concerned for one another. In a free and democratic country all churches are allowed to exist. Each is responsible to God and to the world whom God loved and for whom he died. (John 3:16)

All is not sad and bleak in Nigeria. The Christian population in Nigeria during the last three decades has multiplied. If Christians will speak and act together this increase will enable us to effect great change in our country.

Christian fellowship has been strengthened under the banner of the Christian Association of Nigeria (CAN). CAN makes mutual encouragement and united Christian action possible. Tribalism encourages jealousy, competition, and disunity, but CAN discourages tribalism in favor of unity and strength.

Nigeria reminds me of the havoc at the Old Testament Tower of Babel where people could no longer speak to or hear each other. But in the New Testament, Jesus overcame that problem for us. We have become new people in Jesus Christ, and he gave us a new language of love and unity. Too often though, we insist that our tribe and our own language are superior to all others. That attitude in a country where more than 300 tribes and languages must live together can produce only chaos.

We must also strongly encourage the use of English, our official national language. A common language is essential to an understanding of one another. English should become more than merely our "official" language; none of our more than 200 languages can be adopted as a national language. We must encourage English to become Nigeria's everyday language — in our conversations, schools, churches, and more. Every Nigerian child should learn it well, speak it fluently, and use it as his first language — for the sake of the country itself and for its need to be part of the global community. Meanwhile, our government is destroying the very foundation of a sound, national education system.

Understanding each other is critical. Without it, overcoming tribalism is hopeless. Let us begin with ourselves. We cannot overcome hate if our hearts are hate-filled. Only when our hearts and minds are transformed can we Christians be truly productive, especially in the arena of government.

I urge you, brothers, in view of God's mercy, ... do not conform any longer to the pattern of this world, but be transformed by the renewing of your mind. Then you will be able to test and approve what God's will is — his good, pleasing, and perfect will. (Ro. 12:1,2)

We must begin in our hearts and homes, on our own compounds, in our churches, in our own villages and towns, in our tribes — and among our tribes.

Overcoming tribalism and forging Christian unity alone will not match Islam's present power in Nigeria. I know that. Our unity must produce action, and that is my second point. We need involvement and action in politics as well. We need to become righteously and vigorously angry at the corruption in the government and enraged at the devious attempts of Islam to control Nigeria.

I am troubled that many Nigerians, both Christians and non-Christians, seem oblivious to the rottenness in most of Nigeria's social, economic, political, and spiritual life since our independence. A country is no better than the persons who run the government. Each leader must be honest, dedicated, and strong. Christians must think honestly about their abilities to serve in politics and government. Of course, they will make errors. Errors happen. Some are unavoidable. This should not stand in the way of progress nor hinder Christians from becoming active. The masses have a potentially inexhaustible enthusiasm for social change. They are ready for change and are ready to back the silent revolution that is beginning to ripen. Christians must seize the day!

We fool ourselves badly if we think politics and government do not affect our everyday lives. Freedom to build churches, sending our children to excellent schools, drinking clean water ... must I say more? Would millions of women have to walk miles to draw dirty water from a polluted river if our government had as its highest priorities to provide the nation with clean, pure water and better living conditions, rather than lining its own pockets with dirty money? Churches may never stand in the way. But they do. They fail to challenge their members to political action and leadership. Sometimes they even discourage intelligent, dedicated Christians who might otherwise enter politics. I have listened to many pastors and bishops preach against Christians participating in politics — because "politics is sin," they say. False. False. This critical misunderstanding of politics has kept too many Christians from becoming involved. How sad! In so doing we abandon our fate to unjust, unscrupulous leaders.

One has only to look at the many models of honest Christians and politicians. Many have contributed much to Nigeria and have not fallen from their faith or high standards of servanthood to the people. Quite the contrary, many have grown.

When we use phrases such as "church and society" or "church in society," we do not mean individual churches and denominations but the church as an integral part of society. Its Founder, our Lord and Savior, calls her members "the light of the world," the salt of the earth, a city set upon a hill that cannot be hidden, a chosen generation, a royal priesthood, a holy nation. It cannot be that when it is hunched timidly behind political roadblocks! God calls his people to serve in his kingdom — of which Nigeria is part — using the talents and abilities he has entrusted to them. Nigeria makes this impossible when it discriminates against Christians and prevents them from holding governmental offices.

Applying Christian principles and living a Christian life are difficult even in the best of circumstances. In politics it is even more so. Christians are not immune to the temptations of pride, greed for personal ill-gotten wealth, corruption, falsehood and worldliness. But we must fight them. Valuing each human being as the image of God and valuing the principles of honesty, justice, and mercy are the basic ingredients needed for leaders in power and government. Speaking out against government is hazardous in Nigeria. But remaining silent is hazardous to the country.

We must look at Nigeria's tomorrow. Our children are our most important resource. We must teach them the precepts of Jesus Christ and capitalize on their youth and idealism. Young men and women are active and vigorous. They are eager to learn and open to vision. Yes, they lack experience, but they can learn from the words, wisdom, and actions of older, experienced adults.

The despotism of Nigeria's government today requires that Christians ask, "Are we willing to suffer for doing right?" Early Christians suffered heavy persecution. Can we stand persecution and suffering today — for Christ's sake? Can we accept hardship as Paul and others did? Jesus tells us not to expect that we will be treated differently than he was. He said "The servant is not greater than his lord …. If they have persecuted me, they will persecute you. (John 15:20)

The Apostle Peter said: Happy are you if you are insulted because you are Christ's followers; this means that the glorious spirit, the spirit of God, is resting on you. If any of you suffers, it must not be because he is a murderer or a thief or a criminal or meddles in other peoples affairs. (1 Pe. 4:14)

But, if you endure suffering even when you have done right, God will bless you for it. (1 Pe. 1:20)

You ask, "How can we love those who have killed our people? How can we bless those who have burned our churches? How can we love those who discriminate against us because of our faith? Who deny us contracts? Employment? Promotions? Who even deny us some of our basic rights because we affirm our beliefs? Who deprive us of our right to worship as we believe?"

Burning questions, these. We cannot brush them aside. In spite of gross injustice and unfairness, Christ requires that we love our enemies. God teaches us even to be joyful in times of trouble. Hard words. During times of trial patience — not passion — is set to work in us, whatever we say or do. And patient we must be! "Love your enemies and pray for those who persecute you [or burn your churches and your properties or kill your brethren]." (Mt. 5:44)

Flagrant abuse of power must be corrected within the concepts of Christianity. Zechariah said, "Not by power, nor by might, but by my Spirit, says the Lord." (4:6)

Won't the Muslims construe our patience as weakness? Maybe. We solemnly affirm our faith and vow to practice our Lord's teachings, and when attacked we will defend ourselves and our faith. We are responsible citizens; we are law-abiding; we are loyal. Whether the government be good or bad, we "give to Caesar what is Caesar's and to God what is God's."

We cannot ignore the power of the military and its appetite for more. We cannot ignore the power of Islam and its hunger for more. Nigeria is a democracy. A very shaky democracy. It has enough wealth and opportunity to satisfy everybody's need but not everyone's greed.

The days and years ahead for Nigerian Christians are perilous, but not without hope. We are messengers of Good News and good news for Nigeria.

We have a choice: we can crouch passively behind the roadblock with fear-filled silence or we can unite to break down the roadblock and march ahead towards a people-elected, honest government and restoring democracy for all our citizens.

Which one will we choose?

Let us first join hands and hearts, united together in Christ.

Then we must speak clearly and loudly. With one voice, the voice of Christianity.

Then we must act decisively and powerfully.

Christians and churches, with Jesus as our Savior and also as our King we can help our beloved land to overcome corruption and despotism and clear the way for a free, united, and righteous Nigeria.

Dear God, help us.

Afterword

To my Nigerian fellow Christians and friends,

Besides the daily reading of your Bible, which must always be your Number One book, you should read Exodus 20–23 (the Ten Commandments and other laws) as often as you can, and you should obey God's commandments.

> *God, through Jesus Christ, also said,*
> *A new command I give you:*
> *love one another.*
> *As I have loved you,*
> *so you must love one another.*
> *By this all men will know*
> *that you are my disciples,*
> *if you love one another.*
> *— John 13:34*

My prayer is that you should also love your children the way I love you. If that is done you will have done a marvelous service expected of good children of God. For the Almighty God sees everywhere and will reward and bless each of you according to your behavior.

When the inevitable strikes, you should remain calm and united. Sorrow and silence are strong, and trust, patience, and endurance are godly. In happy homes the light of household fires gleam warm and bright.

For all of us there will always be the beginning and the end.

Appendix

Adaptation of Zaria Provincial Commissioner Jolly Tanko Yusuf's farewell Letter to the People of Wukari Division, September, 1965.

Your Highness, Chiefs, and People of Wukari Division,

I am both sad and happy in writing this letter. Sad because I must say good-bye to my beloved chiefs and brothers and sisters whom I had the privilege to represent in the Northern House of Assembly since 1956. Happy because I am going to the United Kingdom to represent Northern Nigeria as Agent General. I hope you will excuse me if, in my endeavor to thank you for your kindness and cooperation during my tenure of office, both as your representative and as your son, I fail to meet your aspiration.

I thank all of you. Words are inadequate to express my gratitude, not only for your votes during the 1956 and 1961 general elections, but also for your implicit confidence, faith and support, particularly during the historical period 1962–1965, during which I was your Provincial Commissioner. In spite of the difficulties during that time, I will always regard that opportunity as one of the most valuable treasures of my life and my tribe.

I assure you that it was with much careful consideration that I made up my mind to quit active politics, a field where I have been so happy and have made so many friends. But, brethren, you will agree with me that opportunity comes but seldom, and I felt it would be silly to let this opportunity slip away.

I will miss my many good and true friends, and it costs me much to go from brothers and sisters to strangers in a foreign country. It is like leaving a part of myself behind whenever I remember you. Be assured that I shall never forget you no matter how far I may be from home; I love no other place more than this Division.

I feel I shall be doing injustice to the living souls in this Division and to future generations if I conclude this letter without mentioning two important issues: (1) political achievements in the development, employment and education in our area, and (2) unity of purpose, which is the foundation of peace and progress.

I suppose no achievement of which a politician may be more justly proud is greater than the development of a region and the raising of the people's standard of living. The tremendous progress made during the past six years in all fields in this Region (Wukari Division in particular) is a credit to our leaders and to the National People's Congress (NPC).

When the history of Nigeria is written, Wukari Division will occupy the prominent place it deserves because the first chief who represented the people of the area (the so-called Middle Belt) was from Wukari Division and the Jukun tribe. For the interest of youngsters and future generations, I mention the names of a few great leaders.

His Highness Atoshi Agbumanu, king of the Jukuns. Since the introduction of parliamentary rule in 1952, he served in federal and regional cabinets until 1960, when he answered the call of Almighty God. Even though His Highness Atoshi has gone, the history of his service will remain as long as the world exists.

After his death two chiefs from this area were appointed: His Royal Highness Atta of Igala, Alhaji Aliyu Obaje; and the Emir of Ilorin, Alhaji Sulu Gambari. In addition, Chief of Takum His Royal Highness Mallam Audu Amadu, and Chief of Donga His Royal Highness Mallam Muhammadu Sambo also served. Another pioneer, Mallam Ibrahim Sangari Usman, was the first citizen from our area to represent Wukari Division in the Federal Legislature. He served as Parliamentary Secretary from 1954 until 1959. The present political awareness and maturity in our area and Benue Province is due to his untiring efforts.

We have achieved at least some of our political goals and are beginning to build a modern society where the economic wellbeing of our people can continue to improve.

Unity, however, is the true foundation of peace and progress of any nation. Tribalism is false ideology, but it is an ideology that some people use as a political weapon. It can only be fought with spiritual weapons. To win this ideological, tribal battle is neither simple nor easy. We must work extremely hard to persuade our young boys and girls to see the danger of disunity. The battle may last for decades, but by the grace of God it will be won.

The only real hope of any nation is for its people to live together in harmony. If we want a solid foundation for a strong, viable nation, we must do away with tribalism and religious politics. If we want to ensure continued progress in our area and if we want our influence to continue in Nigeria, we must emulate our forefathers. Through unity and cooperation, they conquered most of the present Northern Nigeria long before the establishment of British colonial rule.

If we condemn tribalism, and I am sure we do, I would urge each one of us to begin with self. Accepting the principle that all human beings are created by God in his image is surely the best way to overcome or reduce misunderstanding and hostility in society. We cannot build a society free from hatred if our own hearts are full of hate. We must change, we must love one another. Love is patient. Love is kind. It envies no one. To love in this way requires the spiritual transformation of our hearts and minds and a drastic change in our style of living. We need God-fearing people who will be sincere and honest in their dealings. We need people who will work honestly, lovingly, and patiently towards that goal.

Nigeria needs good, honest, strong leadership, not only in government but also in families and in schools. Elimination of tribalism and sectionalism is a good place to start. The pursuit of restraint and tolerance is also necessary. It is our duty to set moral precedents for children and young people and the generations to come.

Nigeria has enough opportunity to satisfy everyone's need but not everyone's greed. We must continue to cooperate for the desired objective of the development and advancement of Nigerian people for the good of all the people. I look forward to a day when all Nigerians will regard themselves as one family with a single identity — Nigerian.

And, before I stop, I also congratulate you for the able way that you demonstrated political maturity during last Saturday's by-election (September 4, 1965). In spite of internal and external pressure, you voted for our great NPC party in order to safeguard the interest of Northern Nigeria and its people. I pray to Almighty God that you will continue to support the NPC and its leaders.

Good-bye. I hope to come back again if it is the wish of Almighty God.

Index

Colophon

Cover and interior pages designed by
Aaron Phipps. Type was set 10pt on 3pts
leading. This book was produced on a
Power Macintosh 7100/66 using Quark
XPress 3.31 and Adobe Photoshop 3.0.
Electronic pages were impositioned to
film by Electronic Publishing Center.

M C M X C V